The

Sodfather

A Friend of Agriculture

by Jim Graham

Three Decades as Commissioner of Agriculture
The Incredible Story of Farm Economy Growth in North Carolina

Published by
The James A. Graham Scholarship Endowment
N. C. State University
Raleigh, NC
1998

Donated to North Carolina public schools, libraries, community colleges and universities by the North Carolina Farm Bureau Federation.

Index

Jim Graham, Friend of Agriculture

Acknowledgments

We express our deep appreciation to Walter R. Davis for a generous gift to publish this book. Proceeds from the sale of this book will go to the James A. Graham Scholarship Endowment at NC State University which provides scholarships for future agricultural leaders.

I am eternally indebted to hundreds of people whose friendship, hard work and support made my story possible. I am especially appreciative to my personal staff whose dedication and loyalty have given my life added meaning: Donna Creech, Weldon Denny, Peter Daniel and Harry Daniel; and to Charles Heatherly for his persistent effort and patience in helping me tell this story.

Printed in the United States of America

ISBN 0-9634559-2-3

Published by
The James A. Graham Scholarship Endowment
N.C. State University
Raleigh, NC
1998

Dedicated
to my wife, and faithful companion for more than a half century,
Helen,
and our daughters
Alice G. Underhill and Laura Connie Brooks

Foreword

This book is about a favorite son of North Carolinians. It is truly his story of the years he moved across North Carolina, ever the advocate of the farmers, their farms, and the food and fiber they produce for all of us.

Jim Graham has always interpreted and advocated the critical role agriculture plays in our lives. He has made us understand why keeping the land green, the water pure and the farms profitable has so much to do with the quality of life we all enjoy. His years as our Commissioner have been volatile, sometimes controversial, but always years of important growth and lasting achievement.

I first met the Commissioner when he entered NC State as a new student. From then until now, and for more than a half century, I have watched him grow and gather strength and power as a leader in our state. Having been privileged to be his friend and colleague, I know that his energies and dedications have been spent building a greater state and for that uncommon spirit and commitment, we owe him our profound gratitude.

These pages, then, are a visit with this good and gentle man in the broad rimmed hat, who like the great State Fair he has built, has become a legend in his own time.

William Friday

Chapel Hill, NC
Summer 1997

Chapter 1

I Love My Job

"Those who labor in the earth are the chosen people of God."
Thomas Jefferson

In looking back over my long life, a brief speck in the history of time, I am amazed at the change that has occurred on the North Carolina farm in the span of just one generation.

It would be an understatement to say I love my job. The 34 years I've spent as North Carolina's Commissioner of Agriculture have been filled with happy and rewarding experiences. I have enjoyed the work.

I have stomped grapes at the Celebrity Grape Stomping and Scuppernong Tasting Festival. I have thrown bales of hay at the Old Threshers' Reunion in Denton. I've gnawed corn at the State Fair. I've traded laughs with four Presidents and shared cigars with every North Carolina Governor since 1960. And, best of all, I've had my picture taken with lots of pretty girls. However, I've never forgotten who I work for and that is the people of North Carolina, especially the farmers.

I take great pride, along with thousands of other citizens of this great state who have tilled the soil, sown the seed and cultivated the bountiful harvest, year after year, in our accomplishments. Among the major accomplishments is a thriving, diversified agriculture economy in North Carolina that feeds our people and is the envy of much of the rest of the nation.

Cash farm income has increased during my tenure as Commissioner from just over $1 billion a year to just under $8 billion now. As result of their industry and thrift, North Carolina farmers earn the third highest net farm income in the nation. In addition, agri-business ventures account for some $42 billion worth of economic activity. The past three decades have been the most exciting and productive period in the history of North Carolina agriculture. I am proud to have been a part of this era.

To get this job and to keep it, I have run in and won nine statewide campaigns. Each has been a wonderful and memorable experience. I am deeply appreciative to the people of North Carlina for their confidence and faith in me. Those campaigns have provided me with many rich and enduring memories which I treasure today. It was during my first campaign with Dan Moore, before he became Governor, that I yelled my first "donkey bray," a story I shall tell later. With Jimmy Carter watching, in Winston-Salem, I cut loose with a bray that was heard around the world. Meeting with Democrats in Sampson County, near the little Town of Turkey, I got so excited during a speech, gesturing and carrying on that I kicked a door completely off its hinges.

All that I have done in the past three decades and some four years, has been done to advance the cause of agriculture. I have spent my every waken hour striving to improve the lot of the farmer, to improve his livelihood, to guarantee a stable supply of food and fiber at a reasonable cost for the consumer and to improve the quality of life for all of our citizens.

My Story

If I sound as if I know the North Carolina farmer, I do. I know him well. I was born on a North Carolina farm and the earliest sound I remember, next to the gentle voice of my mother was the familiar farm sounds -- the crow of the rooster announcing a new day, the cow's moo at milking time and the bray of a stubborn mule unwilling to put his shoulder to the load.

I come from a long line of farmers. My father was a farmer, as was his father. For seven generations, my forebears were all farmers. They were also Presbyterians and all belonged to the Third Creek Presbyterian Church in Rowan County. They also all bore the given name, "James." And after the Democratic Party was formed, they were all Democrats.

There was never a time in my life when I considered any other choice for my life's work than to be a farmer or to pursue an avocation where I could serve the farmer. The great joy of my life, other than my wonderful family, is that I have been able to do what I set out to do as a young man.

As a teenager, still in high school, I resolved that one day I would be Commissioner of Agriculture of North Carolina and that I would devote my life's work to the important task of helping solve the great problems that perpetually plagued the farmer. I count among my many blessings the good fortune I have had in being able to achieve that goal. This advice I would offer a young man or woman today about to embark upon life's journey: Decide early what you want to do with your life. Make a plan and stick to it. You will achieve so much more if you know what you want to do and devote your life to fulfilling that goal.

Roots in Rowan County

I was born April 7, 1921, in the town of Cleveland in Rowan County, formed in 1753 from Anson. My home county was named in honor of Matthew Rowan, a leader of our state before the American Revolution. Mr. Rowan served briefly as acting governor after the death in office of Governor Gabriel Johnston.

My first thought about becoming Commissioner of Agriculture occurred, or rather was suggested to me, on the farm where I grew up. A hired hand and I were unloading 200-pound bags of fertilizer one day and he read the name of William Graham, then Commissioner of Agriculture, which was printed on the fertilizer. He told me, almost in jest, "Jim, If I were you, I would be Commissioner of Agriculture when you grow up and you won't have to lift these heavy bags anymore."

I was 14 years old and didn't weigh 120 pounds. That idea appealed to me and I thought about it from time to time. It was a sobering thought but one which stayed with me. Mr. William A. Graham served as Commissioner 15 years and was followed in the office by his son, William A Graham, Jr., who served 14 years. They were both fine men but of no kin to my side of the Graham family, as far as I've been able to determine.

Farming was a hard way of life during my childhood, as it is now. It was a good, honest way of life. The work, all done by hand, was physically demanding and dangerous. The hours were long. We didn't have much money but we ate well. Our forebears succeeded and survived in the days before mechanical marvels on the basis of their physical stamina, their personal courage, their enduring faith and their great strength of character.

The early pioneers who first peopled the North Carolina Colony cleared the virgin forests and planted the first crops -- they are the heroes we should honor today because they also planted the seeds of a new generation of hope and opportunity in this land. My ancestors were the proud Scots who came here to escape the oppression of their native land. They brought with them little more than the clothes on their backs and an undying sense of hope. They hoped to find here in this untamed wilderness a place where they could prosper according to their ability and their willingness to work. They hoped to find a place where they could worship, free of interference from the government and free from the tyranny of any other man.

My folks found their place in the western Piedmont of North Carolina, in the wooded, red clay hills of Rowan County. It was not a perfect place, but it was a better place than they had ever been. They stayed there, tilled the soil, planted a crop, started a family, and generation by generation, built a legacy that continues today. That is the story of my family and it is the same story, repeated thousands of times by other fine families who created this great state of North Carolina.

My father was James Turner Graham. He was the first farmer I knew and a good one. He believed strongly in soil conservation. If I heard him say "soil conservation" once, I heard him say it a thousand times. He knew, even in his time without the benefit of a formal education, that if you depended upon the soil for a living, you had to take care of it. He also knew there was a proper role for the government to play in agriculture and, at his knee, I learned of the challenges that faced the farmer.

I had an agriculture teacher, Mr. P.H. Satterwhite, now 94 years old who inspired me and instilled in me strong leadership qualities and an interest in education. After my mother and father, Mr. Satterwhite was the most influential person in my life. He has remained a friend throughout the years. I saw him at every high school class reunion until 1995, which was the first reunion he had missed. In the times of my youth in rural North Carolina a strong agriculture teacher, next to your daddy, was your best friend. Mr.

Satterwhite saw something in me that no one else saw and something I did not see in myself. He encouraged me to go to State College and to get an education that would allow me to reach beyond the horizons that had restrained my father and his generation of farmers. Mr. Satterwhite convinced me that by educating myself, and learning all I could about the scientific farming techniques that were rapidly being developed, I could be a better farmer and accomplish far more than I could ever hope to achieve without such an education. State College was the place to get that education, he said.

My decision to go to North Carolina State University, however, was a disappointment to my mother who saw something else in me. She hoped that I would go to Davidson College and become a Presbyterian minister.

I grew up on a 250 acre farm that, among other things, had 48 head of milk cattle. We grew cotton which cost a penny a pound to pick and sold for a nickel a pound. Also, my father grew grain and hay for the cattle and hogs we raised to eat. He raised horses and mules. My grandfather passed the time in the winter trading horses and mules.

There is a story about two horse traders in those days who frequently swapped with each other. One of them sold a horse to the other for twenty-five dollars and a few weeks later bought it back again for thirty dollars. A few weeks later, the second trader bought the same horse again for thirty-five dollars. This trade, involving the same horse went on for several months until the price got to a hundred dollars. A third trader heard about this phenomenal animal and decided it must be something special. So he went to the farmer who had the horse and bought it for the outrageous price of one hundred fifty dollars. When the original seller came to make his next offer, he was shocked to learn that the horse had been sold to someone else.

"Why on earth did you go and do such a foolish thing as that," he asked. "We were making a good living off that horse."

My First Experience with Hog Cholera

A tragic incident in my childhood became a great influence in my life. I came home from school one day and found my mother

TOP: Commissioner Graham with daughters, Connie Brooks (left) and Alice Underhill. CENTER: My Family: (L-R) My brother, Charles, and his wife, Katherine: my wife, Helen; my mother, Laura: me, my father, James Turner Graham, and my sister, Mary Emma Little. LEFT: Me in 1946 as I began work for the N. C. Department of Agriculture as manager of the Ashe County Research Station.

TOP: The Graham Family--Front Row: (l-r) Connie Brooks, Lauren Brooks, Helen, Jim, Allen Brooks and Alice Underhill. Back Row: Berry Brooks holding Grace Ann Brooks, Berry Brooks, Graham Underhill, Laura Underhill, Reed Underhill and Tee Underhill. CENTER: Helen and Jim; Parents: Laura Allen and James Turner Graham. LEFT: Commissioner Graham with father, and Governor Robert Scott at an event in Raleigh.

in tears. All of our hogs had died of what then was commonly called "swine fever." It was hog cholera and there was no cure for it. In addition to our family, four other families on the farm depended on the hogs we grew for a major portion of our meat for the entire year. That was really a hard blow. Losing those hogs meant that five families would have no pork for an entire year. There was no other place to get hog meat because everybody's hogs died. And even if there had been other meat to buy, we could not have afforded it because this occurred during the Great Depression and nobody had any money.

The next year after the hogs died of cholera, the boll weevil came and destroyed the cotton crop. I vowed then that I would try to find a way to eliminate these and other pests which wiped out many farmers. I have been blessed to have had a part in achieving both of those goals -- eradicating the boll weevil and finding a cure for hog cholera.

My father was a great believer in the land. He believed strongly in six things -- the Presbyterian Church, his family, the Democratic Party, water, soil conservation and good horses. He was a progressive farmer in his day. He was responsible for dredging Third Creek in Rowan County, one of the first inland dredging projects in North Carolina. It was called Third Creek Watershed Project.

I heard my father talk more about soil conservation than any other thing. He told me many times about the importance of taking care of the land. He was one of the founders and a member of the original board of directors of Coble Dairy.

I was the oldest of three children. My brother, Charles, now deceased, farmed the homeplace, went to Appalachian State University, played football and carried the mail. Charles had two children, Kathy and Charles, Jr. My sister, Mary Emma, also now deceased, graduated from then-called Woman's College in Greensboro. She married E.L. Little, who has three degrees, a bachelor of science, a master's degree and a Ph.D. from MIT. He worked for DuPont. They had two children, Jay, now on the faculty of Delaware Community Technical College, and Laura, a member of the law faculty at Temple University. She graduated at the top of her class and clerked for Chief Justice William Renquist.

My mother was a stern disciplinarian. She instilled in us a strong work ethic. She wanted me to go to Davidson College and become a minister. However, even then I had already decided what I wanted to do in life. After getting a degree in agriculture from NC State University, then called State College, I planned to become an agriculture teacher. Then I wanted to be Superintendent of a "Test Farm." Next, I planned to become Commissioner of Agriculture. That was the life's work I had laid out for myself at the time I graduated from high school. I have been blessed by the Grace of God to achieve it all.

Farming During the Great Depression

The typical day on the farm of my youth began at 5 a.m. My brother and I slept upstairs and when Daddy knocked on the bottom of the steps, you had better come out of there. He didn't call twice and most certainly he didn't come up the stairs to awaken us. I don't know what would have happened if we hadn't responded promptly to his knock at the foot of the steps. What he might have done probably would have been called child abuse today but it made a man out of me. One morning, I had been out all night possum hunting and sneaked back into the house just as my father was getting up to start the daily chores. I tried to be cute by quoting an old adage, "A big possum walks before light." My father was not amused. He said, "Big possum, little possum, middle possum. It doesn't matter which. You get yourself out to the barn and get to the work."

I fed and milked the cattle, ate breakfast and went to school. We lived just inside the school bus zone, not quite a mile away. There was a rule then that you had to live more than a mile away from school to ride the bus. After getting up well before dawn and doing chores for three hours, my brother, sister and I walked nearly a mile to school each day in all kinds of weather until I got a bicycle and then I rode to school in a manner of speaking.

My introduction to State College came during a major event at our school. It was the annual Future Farmers of America (FFA) banquet. I was FFA chapter president when Dr. T.E. Brown from Raleigh came up to our banquet and he said, "Jimmy, we want you to come to State College." That settled it.

In high school, I played football, basketball and tried to play baseball. However, I had injured my left eye in the fifth grade by igniting a firecracker in a tin can close to my face. The accident caused a complete loss of sight in my left eye. I was not very good at baseball because I always struck out.

At State College, I went out for football and I will never forget what Coach Herman Hickman told me. He looked at me and said, "Boy, you've got big shoes and big ears. If you ever fill out those ears and those shoes, you will be a heck of a man but you are a long way off." That was the end of my college football career. I wasn't very good in football in high school but I tried.

At State, I made it my goal to know everybody in my class by name. I accomplished that goal. I did that because I wanted to meet as many different people as I could. One reason that I came to know everybody was I delivered the newspaper published by the School of Agriculture, the *Agriculturist.* I had to know not only their names but where they lived. Bill Friday referred to me in his biography as a "politician." He was a year ahead of me and quite a politician, too, though a better one and a smoother one than me. Bill Friday and I have been lifelong friends and I have valued his counsel highly. As President of the University of North Carolina during a period of its greatest achievement, he has become one of our greatest citizens.

At State, I learned about the scientific basics of farming--the pH of soil, and other advanced techniques. It was amazing to confront all of the knowledge which was being discovered about this simple way of life into which I had been born. It was fascinating and exciting.

I also joined the Reserve Officer Training Corps (ROTC); however, my military career was brief. I kept them from knowing about my bad eye by memorizing the eye chart while using my good, right eye and then reading it back from memory. When World War II broke out, I volunteered for active duty but they discovered my eye problem during the physical examination and sent me home.

After graduation, I got a job as the vocational agriculture teacher at the Celeste Henkle School in Iredell County. The school, named for a lady who had been Superintendent of Schools, consisted of grades one through eleven which was as high as public schools went in those days. Also, I coached baseball and basketball. During the three and a half years I taught school, I had several job offers but something kept telling me to stay with the plan I had laid out for myself earlier -- teaching, head a test farm and then onto the job as North Carolina's Commissioner of Agriculture.

I had my eye on a test farm in Statesville but the state sold it. A new farm was established in Ashe County to focus on beef cattle and sheep, and I got the job with the help of Congressman R.L. Doughton and then Commissioner of Agriculture W. Kerr Scott. Another person who became a major influence in my life, and a good friend, was Dr. D. W. Colvard, who served as superintendent of the Old Mountain Test Farm, and later was head of the Animal Science Department at N. C. State University.

We stayed at the Ashe County Test Farm six years, living on the farm there in one of the nicest houses my wife, Helen, and I ever lived in. Helen wasn't very happy there because the place was so isolated and the winters were brutally cold. I remember one year it was so cold and it snowed so much that the ground was frozen until March. I still have fond memories of that place, among them the births of our daughters, Alice and Connie.

On the farm, we conducted a variety of experiments and one I remember well was a test we did in the winter to see whether cattle that stayed indoors and were sheltered from the cold did better than animals which remained outside. We kept one group of cattle in a barn, fed them grain and pampered them all winter. However, the ones that stayed outside and were exposed to the harsh winter blizzards actually outperformed the indoor animals considerably. That taught me that nature has a plan for its creatures.

Another experiment conducted at the farm was about the merits of an early hay cut versus a late cut. We found that the early cut had more nutrition.

I really enjoyed living in the mountains. Those people are really good people once they get to know you; however, it took some time warming up to them. I remember a Mr. McNeil who ran a country store and thought the idea of a state-operated test farm was a silly and wasteful notion. He told me he got all the information he needed from the bulletins that were published by State College. I asked him where he thought the information in those bulletins came from. When he said he didn't know, I told him that information came from test farms such as the one I operated down the road from his store. After that, he was friendly.

Dr. B.B. Dougherty, the legendary founder of Appalachian State University, then of course, just an humble teachers college, was skeptical of the test farm so close to his college. One day he came walking up the road to see what was going on. I remember it vividly because we were putting up hay on the third day of July and it was hot. I don't know how he got there. I never saw his car but I don't think he walked the entire 35 miles from Boone. I showed him around and explained what we were doing and he warmed up to the idea too, apparently after being convinced we weren't going to interfere with what he was doing at Appalachian.

Those mountain people I came to know are the most generous people in the world. I remember a lady who lived back at the head of one of those coves. During a terrible winter, after it had been snowing and sleeting for several days, some neighbors took her some food and when they knocked on her door, and told her they had brought her some groceries, she mistook them for solicitors. She apologized for not having anything to give them, saying it had been a bad winter and she had already used up her supplies, otherwise she would be happy to share what she had.

Because of its isolation from the rest of the state and because its brutally cold winters, that region used to be known as the last province.

After six years at the mountain test farm, I was hired as manager of the Dixie Classic Fair at Winston-Salem and also headed up the North Carolina Hereford Association. I made an overture to become L.Y. Ballentine's assistant commissioner of Agriculture but that didn't work out so I decided to continue to prepare myself. Mr. Ballentine had been Lieutenant Governor before he moved over to the Commissioner's post. When he realized in 1948 that he did not have much of a chance to become Governor, he filed for Commissioner of Agriculture.

In 1957, I left Winston-Salem and moved to Raleigh to become manager of the Farmers Market. That was a risky move because there was an effort underway then to do away with tobacco and replace it with beef cattle and vegetable crops. Anybody who knows anything about the nature of farming in Eastern North Carolina knows that you cannot transform a tobacco farm into a vegetable truck farm. After I came to Raleigh and realized the downside to such a major job of trying to negotiate between the large and small farmers, that move seemed like one of the dumbest things I ever did. In fact, taking advantage of that opportunity was one of the smartest decisions I ever made.

I kept up my interest in politics. I supported Terry Sanford for Governor and when Mr. Ballentine died in office, in July of 1964, Governor Sanford appointed me to fill out his term. Bob Scott actually paved the way for me when he decided not to run for the job of Commissioner of Agriculture as his father had done, choosing instead to run for Lieutenant Governor. I am proud to have counted Bob Scott as one of my lifelong friends.

My father and mother came down to see me sworn into office. It was the proudest day of my life. My father said "Okay, son, you've been chasing that mule for a long time, now you ride it."

My father never abandoned his duty as my mentor and my spiritual leader. He called me one day very distressed. "Jimmy, I've been hearing something about you I don't like."

"What have you heard, daddy?" I asked.

"I hear that you've been cussing in public."

"Where in the world did you hear that?" I asked.

"Never mind, where I heard it. But I heard that you were cussing over at the farmer's market. Is that true?"

"Yes, daddy, it's true but this is a hard job, and I lose my cool now and then."

"Well, Jimmy, you weren't raised to cuss in public and I would appreciate it if you would stop."

I was 43 years old when my father scolded me for cussing in public and I have tried hard to control my language since then.

On another occasion, my father called me up and told me I had done something he would never get over. I had joined the Baptist Church, as my wife wished me to do and my father considered that a betrayal of my devout Presbyterian upbringing.

I met Helen while I was a senior at State College. She grew up in Mocksville where her father was a Baptist preacher. One day I saw this picture of a beautiful woman in a display window of a photo studio on Salisbury Street. I inquired about the identity of this beautiful lady and found out that her name was Helen Kirk. More investigation revealed that she was going to be the home economics teacher at a school in Rowan County near where I planned to work and to me that was encouragement enough to pursue a romance that I suspected must have been blessed from above. We have been married 54 years.

Our daughter, Alice, married Reed Underhill and they have three children--Thurlow Reed "Tee", Laura Helen, and James Graham Underhill. Our daughter, Connie, married Berry Brooks and they have four children--Berry; twins, Allen and Lauren and Grace Ann Brooks.

I am proud of my family which has been my greatest source of comfort and strength over the years. I have especially warm memories for my mother who worked hard to see that my brother, sister and I got a college education. She was a leader in the Home Demonstration movement and she was a great cook.

As this is written, Helen was stricken with Alzheimer's disease seven years ago and is confined to our home. Helen and I made a promise to each other during the prime of our youth that should one become disabled the other would strive to the limit of his or her ability to care for the disadvantaged one in our home. I am proud to say that I have kept my promise to Helen and I shall continue to honor that commitment to the end of my days. The Lord has blessed me with the strength to carry on.

Nine Campaigns

The nine campaigns I've run for Commissioner of Agriculture will always remain among the most memorable events of my life. Each campaign has been an exciting and unique experience. The process of putting your name on the ballot and asking voters for their approval is a humbling experience and one that makes most men shrink from the specter of public service. However, I have come to enjoy the process. There is no better way to hold public officials accountable than by the voting booth.

Each campaign brought special memories but none surpasses an event that occurred in 1976 in Wilkes County. We were attending a Democratic Rally in Wilkesboro, the county seat of Wilkes County which had always voted Republican. Local Democrats had a big sign in front of the courthouse which read, "Vote for Jim." There were a lot of "Jims" on the Democratic ticket that year. Jimmy Carter for President. Jim Hunt for Governor. Jimmy Green for Lieutenant Governor. And Jim Graham, for Commissioner of Agriculture. I was impressed. With only a couple of minutes to speak, I wanted to leave a big impression.

They had brought a donkey to the rally and tied it at the rear of the crowd. Just as I got up to speak, the donkey let out a huge bray that caused the audience to laugh profusely.

In a moment of weakness, knowing that Wilkes County had not voted Democratic in a hundred years, I said, 'if you good folks will carry Wilkes County for the Democrats, from the White House to the courthouse and including all the state candidates, I will come back up here and kiss the rear end of that jackass in front of Smithey's Store."

My promise became the rallying cry of Wilkes County Democrats. They took that donkey everywhere with the message, "Let's vote Democratic and see if Jim Graham will keep his promise."

I forgot about the incident until about 3 a.m. on the morning after the election. My phone rang in the middle of the night and it was my friend, John Guglielmi, from Wilkes County. He worked for Holly Farms and was a member of the State Board of Agriculture.

"Guess what happened last night, Commissioner?" John said. "You carried Wilkes County, and so did all the other Democrats. When are you going to come up here and keep your promise?"

I never thought I would live to see the day when Wilkes County voted a straight Democratic ticket but I was happy to see it. It was worth kissing the donkey's rear which I did and I've got a picture to prove that I kept my promise.

The Bray Heard Around the World

Early during my political career, I perfected the "bray" of the jackass and that became my symbol. Contrary to the best advice of my dear wife and my daughters, I frequently gave the donkey "bray" at special events and political rallies. Campaigning once with Jimmy Carter, on a quiet news day, the national news media picked up my bray as a headliner and it was broadcast around the world, I learned later from the cards and letters.

Once during a Democratic Party meeting in Wilson, the Master of Ceremonies, introduced me saying, "And now, our Commissioner of Agriculture will bray." A couple of elderly ladies misunderstood the speaker and thought he said I was going to "pray." They bowed their heads in anticipation, and became very angry when they heard what I did. Later they came up to me and said that donkey bray was the worst thing they ever heard in their entire lives and swore they would never vote for me again.

Times have changed since my first campaign. I doubt if anyone, certainly not in the near future, will serve three decades in this office. It is too big, too complex and too much change.

When I first got into politics, the party organization was much stronger than it is today. Then, a newcomer had to pay his dues and work his or her way up the organization to get the blessings of party leaders for their approval and support in a statewide campaign. That process eliminated most weak characters and it tended to weed out candidates with problems, such as a lack of integrity or sincerity.

Today, anybody with a lot of money or someone who can get other people to donate money can become a formidable candidate overnight. More often than not, the candidate who wins is the candidate with the most money to spend on television advertising, direct mail, consultants and opinion polls. I never took a poll in my early campaigns. Didn't need to. I learned all I needed to know about politicking by talking to the farmer face-to-face and listening to his advice and working twelve to fourteen hours every day. Nowadays, the political process has become a brutal combat in which challengers seek to gain an advantage not by selling themselves or offering a better alternative to the incumbent. Rather, they seek to win by attacking the reputation of the opponent. Campaigning now is dominated by negative advertisements carefully designed to destroy the character of good men and women. I am proud to say that I never did that. I was fortunate to be able to run my own campaign positively, talking about what I had done and what I intended to do if given an opportunity to serve another term.

Sadly, money has become the most important factor in politics today. The politician with the most money and the meanest campaign usually wins. Money now decides the outcomes of most campaigns. The influence of money has reduced the esteem of politicians and office holders among voters.

My political career has been an extremely pleasant and rewarding experience because it allowed me the opportunity to serve the people I love best, the farmers of North Carolina.

The Future of Farming In North Carolina

Despite the great challenges that now face our farmers the future of agriculture has never been brighter. We will solve the problems now confronting us and North Carolina farmers will continue to play an increasingly important role in the vital job of feeding America.

The advance of technology and the application of this knowledge to agriculture has enabled the farmer to live longer, better and more enjoyable lives. Equally important, consumers benefit with good food and fiber, available in ample quantities at a reasonable price. Food accounts for just 10 percent of the family budget today, the lowest food cost in more than a century. Grocery store shelves are always stocked with a wide variety of healthy, wholesome and delectable products. Nowhere has the advance of technology had a more significant impact than agriculture.

We've witnessed greater agricultural progress in North Carolina, and throughout the nation, in the past three decades than occurred in the previous three centuries. I believe that progress will continue.

To understand how the typical farmer might appear in the next generation, or perhaps this time in the next century, a mathematician might draw a line at the threshold of the previous two centuries and extend it forward for another one hundred years.

The ramifications of such a projection are implausible. Will we be able to control the weather so that the frequency, timing and intensity of rainfall is dictated by crop needs? Will we be able to predict more accurately the demands and needs of consumers so that commodity production can be adjusted accordingly, avoiding the wide swings in supply and demand that have frustrated both farmers and consumers in the past with alternate cycles of feast-to-famine gyrations? And, will we achieve a balance between the rapid growth of certain commodities--such as hogs--and the increased stress they place upon the environment?

I think the answer to all of these questions is an unqualified "yes." And, I envy the young man and young woman today who commits his and her life to the wonderful calling of farming.

In this century, we've progressed from where the typical farmer and his adolescent family toiled sunup to dark just to feed his family to today's achievement where a mere two percent of the population feed the rest. In addition, there is an abundant surplus of farm exports that are responsible for our nation's largest trade surplus.

In North Carolina, total cash farm income has increased since 1900 from a few thousand dollars a year to nearly $8 billion a year. North Carolina farmers now enjoy the enviable distinction of earning the third highest net farm income in the nation. That achievement has brought an unprecedented era of prosperity to the farmer and his family. This progress also has benefitted the consumer.

If the grandsons of today's farmers enjoy a proportionate leap forward in mechanized machinery, disease and pest control and plant productivity gains as did their ancestors in the 20th century, the lifetime of the future farmer will be awesome. When I grew up, the son of a farmer on a Rowan County dairy farm, the mule and horse were our primary source of energy, outside the sweat and toil from my mother, father and siblings. Even at the time I became Commissioner of Agriculture in 1964, we looked at the new tractors, mere babes in the woods compared with today's modern equipment, and marveled at the great progress of technology. In my time, farmers have progressed from the use of manpower, horsepower, steampower to the point now where most work, at least most of the hard manual labor, is done by machines.

The science of farming will become even more advanced and more precise. Already, farmers are using computer and satellite technology to determine when to plant with great accuracy.

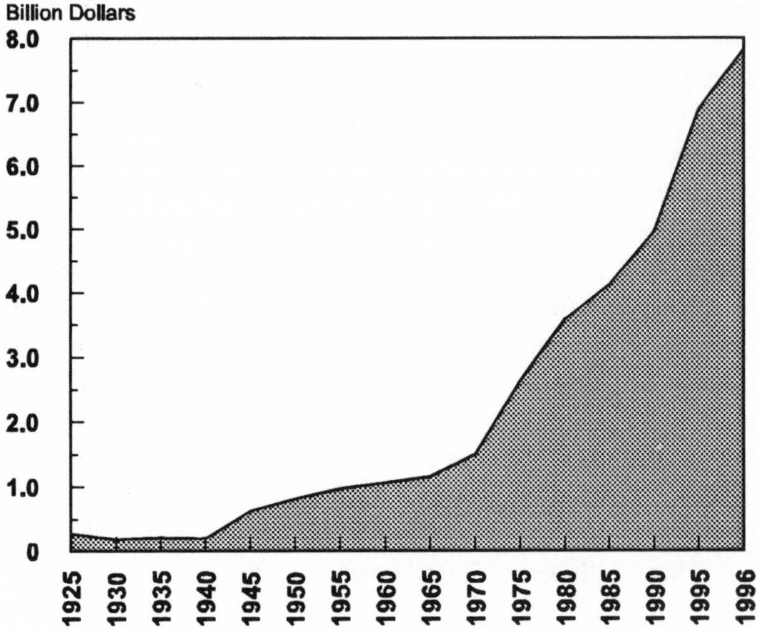

North Carolina Cash Farm Income 1925-96
Table 1

Within the span of a single generation, we have advanced from the mule to satellite technology and we've only begun to tap the vast power of science applied to agriculture technology. Silcon chips, not human brains now determine the right amount and the kind of nutrients. And they say progress will be even faster in the future.

Predictions

Here are some of my thoughts about the forces that will affect and shape the future farm.

The average farm will get larger and there will be fewer farmers. While I have been a strong advocate of the small family farmer--and I hate to see this great icon of our country's rich heritage fade into the twilight of a new century--it is a sad fact that bigger farms are going to prevail. Between 1800 and 1900 the population of this country had increased from just over five million to 76 million. In 1900 the nation's farm population totaled 29.4 million and the number of individual farms (5.7 million) exceeded the nation's total population a century earlier. The average farm nationwide in 1900 was 143 acres.

Today's nationwide farm population is just 4.5 million and that number has shrunk 50 percent in the past 25 years. Meanwhile the average farm size has grown to 471 acres. In North Carolina, there are 58,000 farms today, one fifth as many as existed in 1900. However, the average North Carolina farm today is 160 acres, twice as large as in 1900. If we assume this trend will continue into the future, it is evident that more of our food and fiber will be produced on larger farms aided by the rapid advances of technology. This trend will benefit the farmer, particularly the big farmer, more than it helps the consumer. The concentration of agricultural production into the control of a half dozen or so giant conglomerates will inevitably result in higher prices at the grocery store. This will necessitate a continuing important role for government.

At the turn of the century the lifespan of the average citizen of this country, and this state, was about 45 years. Today, the average lifespan exceeds 75. Much of that increase is due to the abundance of wholesome and safe food. Consequently, much of the credit for our longer and better lives is due to the farmer.

Technology Advances

Technology will continue to revolutionize the way we farm. By improving the quality of seeds, plant nutrients and by exercising more control over the variables that have greatly influenced the practices of agriculture in the past, the future farmer will be able to exert far more control over his outcomes in the future.

Modern equipment and computer technology already have reduced much hard work and uncertainty that once presented great challenges to the farmer.

Genetic engineering is in the midst of a great revolution to develop better seeds and livestock.

Improved chemicals and organic products will continue to increase the farmer's productivity and enhance his ability to control pests.

North Carolina farmers are already very productive, as evidenced by the fact that the average net income per North Carolina farm averaged some $58,000 in 1996, more than twice the average net farm income ($25,299) nationwide.

New marketing techniques, resulting from business alliances, vertical integration, and more accurate economic forecasts, will take the guesswork out of the disposal of the farmer's produce.

We Will Feed the World

As our farmers become more productive and develop modern and sophisticated management and marketing procedures, we will feed the world. Already, we are called upon to fill the void when Russia's wheat crop fails or when China, the largest nation in the world, cannot feed its people. We have gone to the aid of hundreds of third world countries in times of crisis to relieve their starving masses from certain disaster. No one is more capable than the American farmer of producing surplus food and fiber to enable people of the world to enjoy a healthier and more wholesome diet.

The Changing Role of Government

To be sure, the role of government in American agriculture is changing. I am proud of the great and positive influence that government has had upon agriculture during my life. I can remember with vivid detail the despair on the face of my mother and father in the depth of the Great Depression when our crops were virtually worthless because nobody had money to pay for food or anything else. It was a strong government policy that rescued the farmer and created the greatest farm economy in the history of mankind. I, for one, am not apologetic about what government has done for agriculture. Its impact has been vast. While the government may not play as direct a role in the future in planning, subsidizing and managing the supply of farm commodities as a means of guaranteeing the farmer a fair price for his labor in the future as in the past, a strong government influence will continue.

As long as men and women farm, there will always be a need for government. While most farmers are honest, diligent and conscientious, a few will not abide by the rules. A few unscrupulous operators will behave as they did a century ago when it became necessary to create the North Carolina Department of Agriculture. As farms become bigger and as the productivity of our food and fiber is concentrated into fewer hands, the role of government in regulating, inspecting and protecting the interests of the consumer will become even more important.

The threat of litigation is not enough to guarantee a safe and wholesome food supply. Only the intervention of government can inspire producers to achieve a high standard of ethical behavior.

Government will continue to conceive and fund research in the quest for continued advances in agriculture. This is not something the private sector will choose to do with its profits. Government will continue its search for a disease-free environment for plants, healthy animals and clean rivers.

Protecting the Environment

Protecting the environment will become more important. As our cities and urban communities expand into the countryside, it will become more and more important for farmers and their neighbors to live in harmony. Farmers must do a better job managing their waste products, especially animal wastes, so that no adverse impact from agriculture operations spill into the rivers or evaporate into the air. I have said that for 25 years, as the record will show.

In North Carolina

We have a bright agriculture future in North Carolina with cash farm income now totaling $7.8 billion and the total economic impact of farming and agribusiness exceeding $42 billion, the value of agriculture to the State of North Carolina and its people is significant.

Our geographic location, convenient to the great east coast population centers and a mild climate are important advantages that will continue.

Our universities, in conjunction with our own North Carolina Department of Agriculture scientists and other skilled personnel, will continue to develop new techniques and procedures to enable the farmer to increase productivity, cut costs and produce wholesome food and fiber at a reasonable expense.

Our greatest resource is our people. It is to the diligence, the sweat and toil of the good men and women who cleared the land when it was a wilderness that we owe a great debt of appreciation. Generation after generation of farmers have tilled the soil and built the great civilization that we now enjoy. The first settlers were farmers and we owe them an enduring expression of our appreciation for their work and their sacrifice. The hardships they endured built a legacy that we enjoy today in the form of abundant food and fiber at a reasonable price.

We have made great strides in the past half century, especially in the last three decades, in improving the life of the farmer. I am deeply convinced that for the North Carolina farmer, the best times are yet to come.

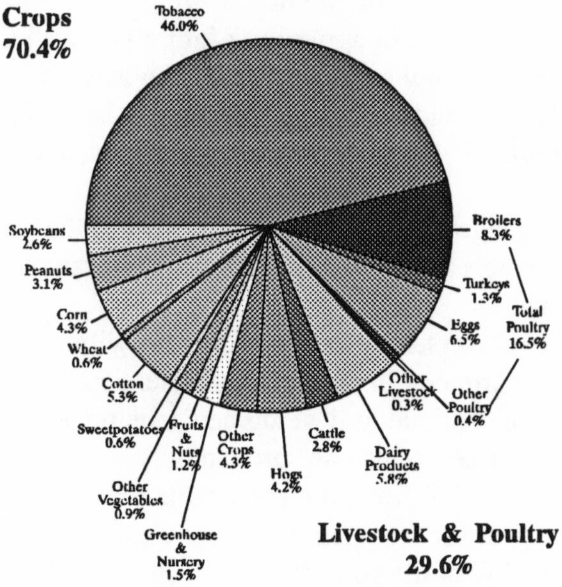

North Carolina Agriculture in 1964
Total Cash Receipts $1.2 Billion
Table 2

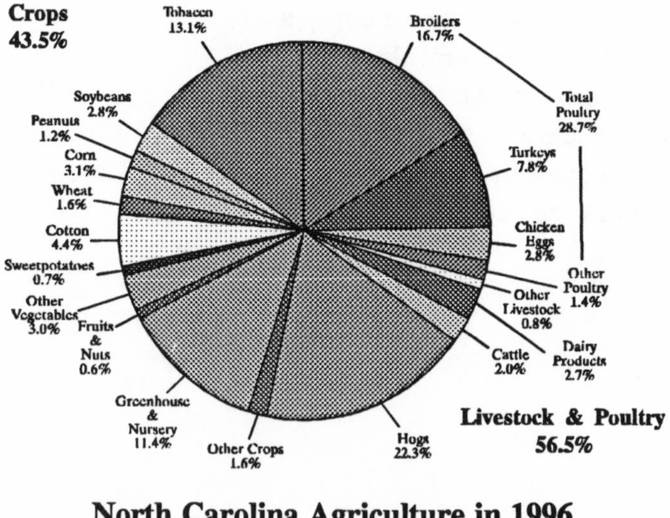

North Carolina Agriculture in 1996
Total Cash Receipts $7.8 Billion
Table 3

Chapter 2

The North Carolina Farmer:
A Profile

Pioneer, Settler, Builder, Planter, Yeoman, Tenant, Conservationist, Scientist, Teacher

"The farmers are the foundation of civilization and prosperity."
Daniel Webster

If you ask me who is the North Carolina farmer and what has he done for our great state, I will tell you this. The farmer built North Carolina. He deserves much of the credit for the necessities, comforts and conveniences we know today. In just this century, our lifespan has increased fifty percent and the quality of our lives has improved immeasurably, largely as the result of agricultural progress. The farmer in North Carolina generates nearly $8 billion worth of cash income annually from his labor. Related commerce and agriculture-dependent industry, such as timber, paper and tobacco manufacturing create agribusiness ventures exceeding $42 billion each year.

A preponderance of North Carolina's agricultural growth has taken place in the past three decades and it can be attributed to three things:

1. The advance of technology and its farm applications.
2. Crop diversification.
3. Aggressive marketing.

I am proud to say some of the credit for these accomplishments belongs to the prudent leadership and loyal stewardship of North Carolina Department of Agriculture employees. Many distinguished citizens have made significant, lifelong contributions to the cause of agricultural progress in North Carolina. Their story deserves to be told.

Technology

There are two components in the advance of technology and its applications to agriculture. First, technological achievements in mechanization vastly increased productivity on the modern farm. When the tractor replaced the farm mule, one man suddenly could do the work of twenty, then forty and now a hundred. Second, scientific advances have given the farmer superior, prolific seed and powerful chemicals to destroy crop pests and eradicate animal disease.

The consumer is the principal beneficiary of this leap in technology as evidenced by the fact that food costs the average family only 10 percent of its budget today. Just a century ago, the typical farmer and his large, extended family worked sun-up to sun-down just to feed his family.

Diversification

The result of crop diversification can be seen from the comparison of statistics between 1960 and 1994 (see Table 2). The story is quite simple. As recently as 1960 tobacco accounted for almost one out of every two dollars of cash farm income. Three decades later tobacco accounts for more than a billion dollars in North Carolina farm sales but today it represents just one out of every seven dollars of farm income. Already, sales from hogs and poultry each exceeds tobacco income. We have made great strides in diversifying our cash crops and that is the solid foundation upon which the future of farming in North Carolina depends.

Marketing

None of these achievements would have been meaningful without an aggressive marketing initiative, largely by the North Carolina Department of Agriculture, which sought to create demand for existing and potential North Carolina products. Much progress has been made in marketing strawberries, sweet potatoes, Irish potatoes, poultry and pork products.

In 1995, some 80 loads of Irish potatoes grown in eastern North Carolina were shipped to Canada under a special agreement negotiated by our Department and Canadian customs officials. Without that agreement and the advance sales, those potatoes would never have been planted.

The Typical Farmer

The North Carolina farmer today is light years ahead of his colonial contemporary in the way he works. Equipped with an array of modern technology and an advanced body of knowledge, today's farmer produces a sufficient quantity of food for himself and 130 other people. He still works daylight to dark at certain peak times; however, mechanization has brought him the tools which allow planting, cultivation and harvesting to be done with only a fraction of the manual labor required just a generation ago. With this advanced know-how, our farmer stands out, a giant among his peers across the nation.

There are 58,000 farms in North Carolina today. The typical farmer is 55 years old, or to be precise, 54.7 years as the U.S. Census Bureau found in 1992. There are only one fifth as many farms in North Carolina today as there were at the beginning of this century; however, today's Tar Heel farm averages 160 acres each and are twice as large as the typical farm in 1900.

North Carolina leads the nation in the production of tobacco, sweet potatoes and turkeys. We are number two in pickled cucumbers, trout and cash receipts from poultry and egg products.

North Carolina pork producers rank third in the nation and have written a new significance to the old adage "bring home the bacon" as the rapidly growing swine industry promises to become even more important in our state's farming future.

We rank fourth in the production of commercial broilers, peanuts, blueberries and rye; seventh in apples; eighth in chickens (not counting broilers), strawberries, peaches and watermelons; ninth in eggs and tenth in cotton.

In view of the fact that North Carolina ranks 10th in population among all the states, those measures of achievement in which our farmer out performs his peers nationwide is an amazing story of both perspiration and inspiration.

In 1790, some 93 percent of all people in the young nation were farmers and most of their life-long labor, from daylight to dark, was spent providing food and shelter for themselves and their families.

Major NC Farm Commodities

Rank	Item	1996 Cash Receipts (Millions)
1	Hogs	$1,749
2	Broilers	1,310
3	Tobacco	1,021
4	Greenhouse/Nursery	889
5	Turkeys	612
6	Cotton	343
7	Corn	242
8	Chicken Eggs	218
9	Soybeans	217
10	Dairy Products	212
11	Cattle & Calves	154
12	Wheat	123
13	Peanuts	96
14	Sweet potatoes	53
15	Apples	24

North Carolina's Rank in U. S. Agriculture, 1996
Table 4

Today, barely two percent of our population are farmers but they feed the other 98 percent with abundance, quality and dependability. The shelves of America's grocery stores are always stocked with an abundance and great variety of reasonably priced and attractively packaged foodstuffs. Today the typical family spends only 10 percent of its annual budget on food. Sixty years ago food took nearly half the family budget. One hundred years ago almost all of the family productivity, including the labor of several adults, was spent during the growing season sowing, cultivating, harvesting and storing food. That kind of life came to be called "subsistence" farming and it was the only kind of life most of our citizens knew for more than half our country's history.

The First Settlers Were Farmers

With his own hands the farmer cleared the virgin forests and planted a crop to feed his family and livestock. Possessing little more than the clothes on his back, the farmer and his strong-hearted wife overcame immense hardships as they migrated first through rich Coastal Plains, then across the red clay hills of the Piedmont and finally up into the Highlands.

The early Tar Heel farmer lived off the land, supplementing the food he did not grow by picking wild berries, fishing and hunting wild game and fowl. He saw little cash and if he had any money there was not much to buy with it, except more land to till.

Tobacco, because of its demand and because it could be preserved and stored easily, became an early form of exchange. In 1760 a pound of tobacco sold for as much as a bushel of wheat in England, yet cost only a fraction as much to raise and ship.[1]

The farmer grew corn, potatoes and beans for his own table. Cotton and sheep, and the skins of wild game, provided raw materials for his clothing. He read the Bible for his enlightenment and spiritual guidance. His simple log home of hand hewn logs was usually built near a creek or a fresh spring that provided water for drinking, cooking and rare baths. His simple way of life may sound romantic and nostalgic today but it was a brutal existence as reflected by the high rate of infant mortality and a relatively short life-span for those who survived into adulthood.

As the farmer moved westward, he formed towns and communities. Horse paths were widened to accommodate wagons and became roads, linking community and town and county to county. In this manner, the farmer created the building blocks upon which the societal foundation of North Carolina rests today.

---

[1] Edward J. Dies, *Titans of the Soil* (Chapel Hill: North Carolina Press, 1949), p. 14.

The farmer was America's original entrepreneur. He took great risks that placed his own survival in jeopardy. More than any other group, farmers developed and nurtured a set of values that have constituted the norm in public thought and behavior in North Carolina and much of the nation. These values, distilled over the white hot flame of a southern mystique, tempered by a brutal Civil War and flavored with periodic episodes of hard times, came to be known as the "North Carolina Way." They produced a self-sufficient farmer strengthened by adversity and hardened by the reality that he must survive by his own efforts. Although this good way of life, characterized best for its strong work ethic, honesty, integrity and candor mixed with a wry sense of humor, came under siege in the 1960s, our core values established by the early farmer form the preferred lifestyle today for an overwhelming majority of our good rural and urban citizens.

The First Farmer

Our first farmer of note was George Washington, the first President, first commander-in-chief, and, first in the hearts of his countrymen. A decade before the American Revolution, George Washington was part of an unsuccessful effort to drain North Carolina's Great Dismal Swamp and use the rich basin for farming. Washington was an early scientific farmer, carefully rotating his crops and experimenting with primitive ways to prevent soil erosion and to enrich the soil, long before the discovery of chemical fertilizers. At the height of his farming success, Washington's plantation produced 89,000 pounds of tobacco in 1763.[2] Though he died the wealthiest man in America, Washington experienced the cash-starved plight of many farmers as evidenced by the fact he had to borrow money to attend his first inauguration as President.

In his heart, George Washington was a farmer before he was either a soldier or statesman, as he wrote in 1788, the year before he became President: "I am led to reflect how much more delightful to an undebauched mind is the task of making improvements to the

---

[2] Ibid.

earth, than all the vainglory which can be acquired from ravaging it by the most uninterrupted career of conquests." [3]

Blessed by Abundance

When the first English explorers walked ashore on Carolina soil at Roanoke Island, July 26, 1584, the poet among them, Philip Amadas, described what he saw and it was sweet music to the ears of those pioneers who knew they would have to live off the land.

The new land, Amadas wrote, "was clad with vines which reeled so full of grapes as that the very beating and surge of the sea had overflowed them of which we found such plentie as well there as in all places else, both on the sand and on the green soil, on the hills as in the plains, as well as on every little shrub as also climbing towards the tops of the cedars, that I thinke in all the world the like abundance is not to be found."[4]

The Unfriendly Land

North Carolina has become a great farming state in spite of the fact that conditions here were never completely ideal for agriculture. To be sure, our year-round, mild climate with its four distinct seasons is a major advantage and that comes from our location in the temperate zone, lying between 34 degrees and 36.30 degrees north latitude. Most of the great civilizations of the world - the Romans, Greeks, the Egyptians, the Syrians -- have risen around the earth from this same geographic band which features ample rainfall, bright sunshine and a long growing season.

The soil has presented the North Carolina farmer some of his greatest challenges. Except for parts of the lower coastal plain, North Carolina was not blessed with an endless supply of rich, verdant soil. Farmers quickly exhausted the nutrients from their good earth. Not knowing a better way, they abandoned these spent fields and cleared more land to till until those fields, too, were exhausted. The early farmer toiled under the frequently repeated

---

[3] Ibid, p. 13.

[4] James M. Robinson, *A History of Agriculture in North Carolina* (Unpublished manuscript) State Library, Raleigh, NC, p. 2.

and mistaken notion that it was cheaper to buy a new acre than fertilize an old one.

In the mid-1930s, not long after commercial fertilizer became available, the western coastal plain region of North Carolina held the dubious honor of using more fertilizer than any other region in the entire country.

The Farmer Fights To Be Free

Rice and tobacco were important cash crops during the early days of the Carolina Colony with northern farmers favoring large tobacco fields and the southern planters growing rice in the low wetlands. Both crops became valuable trade commodities and sources of contention with merchants in the Mother country who manipulated the trade laws to their advantage.

On April 12, 1776, North Carolina farmers became fed up with unfair trade policies, high taxes, cumbersome regulations and the arrogance of the British monarchy. Assembled in the town of Halifax, then a prosperous farming and trading center on the banks of the Roanoke River, they voted to authorize the North Carolina delegates to the Continental Congress to vote for independence. This was the first declaration of independence by any of the colonies and became a source of inspiration for other oppressed farm leaders.

Such is the history of the North Carolina farmer. His past is inexorably linked to the step-by-step development and progress of the state.

Visitors to the historic town of Halifax today marvel at the knotted and gnarled 200-year old mulberry tree which stands near the site where the Halifax Resolves were enacted by North Carolina's legislative leaders as they embarked upon the first declaration of independence of any of the colonies.

The mulberry tree is the sole survivor of an orchard of its kind that had been planted by prosperous Halifax merchants, hoping to induce the silk worm to propagate and do its work. Unfortunately, this was not the species of mulberry favored by the silk worm and the effort to produce silk in copious quantities failed.

Early colonial records indicate that locally produced silk sold for as much as 25 English pounds per pound. Silk was so significant among the property of Royal Governor Gabriel Johnston that he mentioned it in his will. However, in their dream to create in the new world a source of silk rivaling the fine quality of silk in the Orient, the North Carolina farmers demonstrated a spirit of energy, imagination and scientific curiosity that continues today as a major strength of the Tar Heel character.

In the early 1700's tobacco brought 10 shillings per hundred weight. Indian corn sold for one shilling eight pence per bushel. Wheat was three shillings, eight pence a bushel; butter, six pence a pound; cheese four pence a pound.[5]

Pitch, the raw product from which turpentine was made, brought a pound a barrel and became a very important trade commodity. But the real money to be made was in livestock. A barrel of pork sold for two pounds five pence and a barrel of beef brought one pound and 10 pence.

Hemp was raised in prodigious quantities and sold for six pounds a ton and that was before the young generation began smoking its leaves.

Diversification Comes Slowly

For much of its first two hundred years, North Carolina was a one-crop state, depending largely upon the fortunes of first cotton and then tobacco to provide the cash income that could be harvested from the good earth. There was good news and bad news in this strategy. Good times were very good but the bad times were very bad and the bad times, for most hard working people, seemed to outnumber the good times.

In good times, the farmer did the work and shared the income from his crop with the banker and the merchant. In bad times, the farmer quite often lost his farm and his home to his creditors though the cause of his bad fortune may have been entirely beyond his control, coming from either too much rain, or too little,

---

[5] Ibid, p. 23.

the boll weevil or a hundred other pests that lay in wait for the right moment to attack.

As recently as 1960, tobacco accounted for 49.1 percent of total cash farm income in North Carolina. In 1996, tobacco cash receipts totaled $1 billion and accounted for 13 percent of the state's total farm income.

Cash income from the sale of livestock, dairy and poultry products totaled $4.4 billion in 1996 and exceeded the value of cash receipts from all crops by $1 billion.

Cash income from both hogs and poultry each now exceed tobacco in cash receipts. Hogs are now the number one source of cash farm income in North Carolina. This achievement was possible because of the eradication of hog cholera and brucellosis; more will be said about these two important achievements later.

The comeback of cotton is a remarkable story that has been untold. In 1996, North Carolina farmers planted 721,000 acres of cotton and by the year 2000, I believe, and am hopeful, we will see more than a million acres planted in this crop that once was king of the North Carolina farm. The 1994 cotton crop sold for nearly one dollar a pound, a far sight better than the nickel a pound my father got for his cotton in 1933. Until 1994, cotton had not brought a dollar a pound since the Civil War.

The success of cotton is attributable in large part to the eradication of the boll weevil, a battle in which the North Carolina Department of Agriculture played a major role. It has been my lifelong ambition to eradicate the boll weevil, which we have done in North Carolina. Technology and marketing have played a major role in cotton's success. More about that story later.

A number of other crops have important stories to tell and hold great potential as significant sources of greater farm income in the future.

Marketing

See Chapter 5 for a detailed discussion of the Department's marketing program.

Good Leadership

Much of North Carolina's success in developing its farm economy is due to good leadership by many people in both the public and private sectors. Two of North Carolina's most influential leaders were Leonidas Lafayette Polk, our first Commissioner of Agriculture and the founder of North Carolina State University and W. Kerr Scott who literally got the North Carolina farmer out of the mud with the state's most ambitious farm-to-market road building program of its time.

Polk was responsible in large part for the creation of the Department of Agriculture, and as our first Commissioner, he instituted a plan of work that became the model and basis for those who followed in his footsteps.

Scott, who later became a great governor, conceived a road building program at first opposed by the state's leading financial interests but which resulted in an era of unprecedented growth, not only for agriculture but for industrial development as well.

There are others -- hundreds of hardworking and progressive minded tillers of the soil -- in the private sector whose achievements have been lauded in the North Carolina Agriculture Hall of Fame. Their achievements should not be overlooked.

Dr. Jane Simpson McKimmon, who Governor O. Max Gardner called "the greatest home builder of the state" because of her innovative work and leadership in the field of home demonstration, is one example.

Clarence Poe was not a farmer in the true sense of the word but he probably educated and inspired more good farming than any other member of our generation. Dr. Poe was the student of Leonidas Polk and the son-in-law of North Carolina's first great education governor, Charles Aycock. For 65 years, Dr. Poe edited the *Progressive Farmer Magazine* which became, after the Bible, the most important literary work in rural American homes. Poe, a native of Chatham County, championed the development of rural America. He advocated technology, diversification and marketing, the three achievements which have brought about such great success to agriculture.

Ben Kilgore came to North Carolina from his native Mississippi in 1899 as the State Chemist, a position he held 44 years. During that time he became known throughout the South as its greatest agricultural scientist. He served as the first director of the North Carolina Agricultural Extension Service and as Dean of Agriculture at North Carolina State College. A building at NC State University bears his name today and farmers everywhere will benefit until the end of time by his tireless efforts and numerous scientific achievements.

Summary

The North Carolina farmer survived hardships, uncertain weather and a Spartan existence to build a civilization which we know today as a good way of life. We take too much for granted today, perhaps from a mistaken belief that our grocery shelves will always be stocked with plenty of reasonably priced food. We hope that it will be so but it did not happen by accident and it won't continue without the same combination of hard work, good leadership and intelligent choices that made it happen in the first place.

This is the story of the North Carolina farmer and how he built North Carolina.

Chapter 3

The History
of
Agriculture in North Carolina

"The farmers are the founders of civilization and prosperity."
Daniel Webster

The early history of North Carolina is largely the history of its agriculture. Farming was the prevalent livelihood of the typical Tar Heel family for the first two centuries of this state. Only in the past half century have industrial jobs and employment opportunities in the professions and service sectors been widely available.

It would not be an exaggeration to say that the farmer built North Carolina. In fact, the farmer built North Carolina's economy twice. First, between the time of the original settlement of the colony to the Civil War, it was the farmer who cleared the wilderness and planted tobacco, corn, wheat, beans and rice. Most of what he grew was needed to support his family and other members of his extended family who provided labor.

By the Civil War in 1861, North Carolina had accumulated a great deal of wealth in land, property and produce, largely from the toil of the farmer. The value of all North Carolina crops was estimated at $33.4 million in 1860, a fifty percent increase over the previous decade. Much of that wealth was directly attributed to the tremendous growth in tobacco production between 1850 and 1860 (from 12 million pounds to 33 million pounds per year). This growth resulted largely from the discovery of the bright leaf variety and the artificial curing process which gave the farmer more control and flexibility over the drying operation.

Cotton production also enjoyed a big boost in the years just before the war, rising from 34,617 five-hundred pound bales in

1840 to 73,845 bales in 1850 and to 145,414 bales in 1860.[1] Cotton was bringing the profitable rate of 28 cents a pound just before the war and a few large plantation owners were getting rich while a good many farmers were enjoying their first taste of prosperity.

Almost all of the great agricultural wealth which the state enjoyed in 1860 was consumed either by the war or destroyed by the conquering rogues in the decade of Reconstruction that followed. Beginning in the late 1870s the task of rebuilding North Carolina fell once again upon the back of the farmer and he shouldered this burden without complaint.

The farmer, in my opinion, is the real hero of North Carolina history.

Colonial Period

During the early days of the North Carolina colony, 95 percent of the first settlers were engaged in agriculture, according to historian Hugh Lefler. [2]

Good land was abundant and it was cheap. Land was available for as little as 25 cents an acre and there was so much of it that buyers could not be found at that price. The choice parcels in the rich coastal lowlands were quickly taken by the first settlers. Later arrivals were forced to travel westward to the rolling red clay hills of the Piedmont and then to the mountains.

It has been state policy from the beginning of North Carolina to encourage agriculture as evidenced by the fact that agriculture was discussed by every session of the Colonial Assembly. Bounties were offered for the production of flax, hemp, indigo, silk and several other commodities which could be traded with England.[3] Several farm crops, such as corn, tobacco and wheat were

---

[1] Hugh Talmage Lefler and Albert Ray Newsome, *North Carolina: The History of A Southern State* (Chapel Hill: University of North Carolina Press, 1953) p. 370.

[2] Ibid, p. 82.

[3] Ibid, p. 85.

authorized as a medium of exchange and became a form of "commodity money."[4]

The early farmer did not know about nor did he practice the scientific methods of agriculture which we know today. The same crops were planted in the same fields for several years until the land was exhausted and those fields were abandoned, left to grow over again with pines and hardwoods. New fields were cleared and planted until they were exhausted. Many planters followed the superstitions of their ancestors and plowed, planted and harvested crops according to phases of the moon.

The early farmer was also plagued by an army of bugs, worms, weevils and larger crop predators commonly referred to as "vermin." These so-called "vermin" consisted of crows, wild pigeons, doves, wild turkey, eagles, owls, deer, bear and other wild animals which feasted upon the farmer's produce and his livestock.

In his address to the General Assembly in 1736, Governor Gabriel Johnston advised farmers, "For the better preserving your Cattle, Corn and other grains, I believe you will find it highly necessary to provide a sufficient reward for the killing of vermin which I am informed have done a great Mischief in most parts of the Province."[5] The General Assembly itself offered rewards for a number of the more destructive pests.

The life of the small farmer was not easy. The typical farm averaged between 50 and 100 acres and provided little more than subsistence for the farmer and his family. He cleared a small spot in the forest for his primitive one or two-room cabin which was equipped with the simplest homemade furnishings. Water was furnished by a nearby fresh water spring or a creek. The average North Carolina farmer had no slaves or servants. The rugged life on the frontier encouraged the trend toward large families which meant more willing hands to till the soil. Farmers routinely exchanged labor during the planting and harvest seasons.

They supplemented their grain diet with protein from the wild animals of the forest and fish from the creeks and rivers.

---

[4] Ibid, p. 86.

[5] Ibid, p. 87.

Clothing was homemade from the wool of the native sheep or from the hides of animals.

There was little cash money and few places to spend what money was in circulation. The farmer needed to buy salt and sugar, which was not locally grown and money for these items was obtained by selling hogs or cattle or trading hides and furs. Or he simply traded what he had for what he needed.

As an example of the value of farm produce, in 1780 the General Assembly adopted a new tax policy to raise funds for the Revolutionary War. The legislature enacted new taxes which applied to all citizens of the state. An example of an early tax was the levy of "one peck of Indian corn, which each citizen was required to pay for each one hundred pounds of property he owned, or half peck of wheat, or five pounds of good flour, or one fourth peck of clean oats or three-fourths peck of rye or one peck of rough rice." The good folks of Carteret County were permitted to provide one gallon of salt in payment of their taxes.

The lack of good roads was a major detriment to commercial farming until the early 1900s when Governor Cameron Morrison led the state's first major push to build a statewide road system that connected each of the 100 county seats. In 1842, Governor John Morehead said "it cost half the value of a farmer's crop to transport the other half to market."[6] Because of the expensive transportation costs, flour from inland North Carolina was more expensive to coastal settlers than flour from Baltimore.

In 1816 the total value of all North Carolina produce shipped through the state ports was only $1.3 million.[7]

Life on the North Carolina farm was so harsh that thousands of families abandoned their stakes and left for the hope of a better life somewhere in the west. For a while, North Carolina became known as the "Ireland of America" because of the great exodus of emigrants. During this period an important duty of the Department of Agriculture was the job of recruiting newcomers to the state through its Division of Immigration.

---

[6] Ibid, p. 300.

[7] Ibid.

A state legislative committee reported in 1833 that nine-tenths of the farmers surveyed said they would move away if they could sell their farms.[8] The 1860 Census revealed that some 405,000 North Carolinians (about half of all the free native citizens) were living outside the state. This meant a sharp loss in population, labor, leadership and wealth. Land values declined.

Qualifications for voting and holding office were based on the farmer's wealth. The 1776 State Constitution provided that only male taxpayers could vote for a member of the House of Commons. Owners of 50 or more acres of land could vote for state senators. Only those owning 100 acres or more could be elected to the House of Commons, 300 acres for the State Senate and to be Governor, one had to possess property valued at one thousand pounds or more. Since the General Assembly enacted the laws, elected the Governor and members to the United States Senate, the North Carolina government that prevailed from 1776 until 1836 was by and primarily for the benefit of the large property owners in eastern North Carolina. The 1776 Constitution also specified that two members of the House of Commons and one state senator would be elected from each county, regardless of its size or population. Thus the East dominated North Carolina public policy until the mid-1800s, long after the Piedmont became more populous.

There was a brief effort around 1815 to begin a program of internal improvements, including the development of the state's agricultural potential; however, the movement fizzled due to inadequate funding and the lack of sustained interest on the part of state leaders. One of the most significant developments during the period was a geological survey of the state and publication of its reports in the mid-1820s by two University of North Carolina professors, Denison Olmsted and Elisha Mitchell.

Constitutional reform in 1835 redistributed political power to give the more populous Piedmont greater influence in the General Assembly and with that access to power came a series of internal improvements such as the building of several plank roads and the development of a statewide railroad system which greatly improved transportation.

---

[8] Ibid, p. 306.

The prosperous decade: 1850s

Agriculture prospered during this period and by 1860 the value of North Carolina crops had increased to more than $33 million. Much of this prosperity was due to the success of two major crops, tobacco and cotton. With the development of bright leaf tobacco in the early 1850s the production of tobacco rose to 12 million pounds in 1850 and to 33 million pounds annually a decade later. The new bright leaf brought higher prices and could be cured artificially and quicker than the sun-drying method used for burley tobacco.

Cotton production jumped from 34,000 five-hundred pound bales in 1840 to 74,000 bales in 1850 and to 145,000 bales in 1860.[9] The state's rice crop, produced largely in Brunswick County, totaled eight million pounds in 1860. Corn production totaled 30 million bushels and wheat 4.7 million bushels that year.

With the newfound prosperity came a desire to build a system that would allow the farmer to sustain his success. The State Agricultural Society was formed at Raleigh, October 8, 1852, and held the first annual State Fair the following year. A chair of applied chemistry was established at the University of North Carolina in 1854 and agricultural leaders began to discuss improved methods of farming such as the use of fertilizers, manure, crop rotation, erosion, soil conservation and others.

In 1860, North Carolina ranked first in the South in the production of honey; second in oats, rye, hay and sweet potatoes; third in tobacco, rice, wheat, hogs and Irish potatoes; fourth in sheep; fifth in corn, wool and cattle; sixth in milk cows; seventh in butter; and ninth in cotton.[10]

The 1860 Census reported a total of 48,661 farms in North Carolina with an average size of 316 acres each. Only 311 farms were larger than 1,000 acres and 46,300 were smaller than 100 acres.

---

[9] Ibid, p. 370.

[10] Ibid, p. 379.

The Impact of the Civil War
Upon Agriculture in North Carolina

The Civil War brought great scarcity and even greater hardship to the North Carolina farm. Most able-bodied men between the ages of 18 and 50 were forced into military service. thus leaving most farms unattended.

North Carolina was the only Southern state which clothed its own soldiers. During the war, the state bought the entire output of its 39 textile factories and set up an operation in Raleigh to make uniforms, overcoats, gloves and shoes.

The state established salt factories along the coast to manufacture salt by evaporating sea water; however, the price of salt still escalated to $70 a bushel. Bacon which had sold for 33 cents a pound in 1862 sold for $7.50 a pound in 1865. Wheat sold for $50 a bushel, flour $500 a barrel and coffee $100 a pound.

Human Cost of the War

More than 40,000 North Carolina's best young men died during the war. A capital investment valued at more than $200 million in slavery was abolished. Land values plummeted. Millions of dollars more in railroads, factories, public bridges, school houses, private homes and barns were either destroyed during the war or in badly need of repair when the thousands of surviving farmers returned to their overgrown and run-down farms. Once affluent families were reduced to poverty. Much of that of value which had not been destroyed or consumed during the war was misappropriated or stolen during the corrupt Reconstruction government that continued to loot the state for a decade afterwards.

The poor farmer who had been forced to leave his family to fight a brutal aggressor, if he was fortunate enough to survive the hardships of battle, returned to a state of defeat and despair. It would be his lot in life to start all over again and rebuild this place he called home.

The war stimulated interest in smoking and Washington Duke and his sons exploited this demand with the aggressive expansion of their tobacco manufacturing business in Durham and with a ruthless marketing scheme. By 1904 the value of Duke's American Tobacco Company was estimated at $274 million and it controlled three-fourths of the tobacco market in the entire United States.

Slavery and Sharecropping

Two of the saddest chapters in the history of North Carolina agriculture are the periods when slavery and sharecropping were prevalent. Slavery prevailed in our country for more than 150 years. This evil institution caused and has led to more misery in the human family than any other social event.

In 1860, just before the Civil War began, North Carolina's population of 993,000 included 360,000 Negroes, all but 30,000 of whom were slaves.[11] The vast majority of North Carolina families never owned slaves as shown by the 1860 census which placed the total number of slave holding families at 34,658. Most slaveowners held fewer than five slaves. At the peak of the slave era, just before the Civil War, there were only 113 families in North Carolina who owned a hundred or more slaves.

Though slaveowners represented a small minority of the state's population, they controlled a vast majority of its wealth, and therefore dominated its political power. Nowhere was this imbalance of power felt more sharply than in taxation policies. In 1860, for example, the tax on a $1,000 slave was 80 cents and according to historian Hugh Lefler, about half of the slaves escaped taxation altogether. At the same time, a thousand dollar cash income was taxed at six dollars and a thousand dollars worth of land was taxed at two dollars. A free mechanic and laborer who earned $500 a year had to pay a five-dollar license tax and 80 cents poll tax while the owner of a slave was taxed only 80 cents. This inequity placed the free laborer at a great disadvantage in his attempts to sell his labor and this obviously unfair state tax policy led to great political outrage.

The abolition of slavery resulted in the pouring of some 330,000 former slaves into a labor market where there was little demand for work. Sharecropping, or tenant farming, was the natural outcome. Large plantations and farms were divided into smaller plots tended by former slaves and poor whites for a share

---

[11] Ibid, p. 395.

of the crop. In principle, this idea sounded better than in practice. Tenant farmers seldom made a profit. They were victimized by high costs of seed and interest, unpredictable weather and a host of farm pests. They were exploited by merciless landowners and greedy merchants. Unstable farm prices and the lack of any organized effort to improve agriculture made the practice of farming a chaotic existence until well into the 20th Century.

The one-crop culture--first cotton, then tobacco--led to another misadventure for North Carolina farmers during this period as the tenant farmer was forced by his landlord and creditors to plant as much of his land as possible in the cash-producing crop, thereby leaving little or no opportunity to grow his own food. For a while, North Carolina was actually importing, at extraordinarily high prices, much of the food it was consuming.

In 1925 some 128,000 of North Carolina's 283,000 farms were operated by tenants. Though this practice had continued to flourish for decades and was clearly a major source of widespread ignorance, poverty and misery throughout rural North Carolina no one except for a few professors and Clarence Poe, the courageous editor of the *Progressive Farmer*, spoke out against it.

Samuel Huntington Hobbs, Jr. professor in the Department of Rural Social-Economics at the University of North Carolina wrote in his book, "*North Carolina Economic and Social*" published in 1930, "The greatest single economic and social problem in North Carolina and throughout the South is farm tenancy. With 45.2 percent of her farms operated by tenants, North Carolina is one of the nation's leading farm tenant states."[12]

"Our leading tenant counties should begin to look for some sensible solutions to the tenant problem. If the practice of the last 60 years continues, eastern North Carolina will be a land of few landlords and many tenants. History teaches us the peril of this condition."[13]

---

[12] Samuel Huntington Hobbs, Jr., *North Carolina Economic and Social* (Chapel Hill: University of North Carolina Press, 1930), p. 119.

[13] Ibid, p. 131.

Colonel Leonidas Lafayette Polk
The First Commissioner of Agriculture
1877-1880

"There is one attractive charm inseparable from and peculiar to this section. The lands which once brought into cultivation are now turned out to wash into deep gullies or to grow up in old field pines, but there is a rich, uniform covering of green verdure all through summer. If not sown or planted the whole earth as far as you can see, is hidden by a carpeting of clover and grass, which grows luxuriantly upon the highest knobs. The finest stock, especially cattle, I ever saw. Everyone has his milk house, through which pours, in abundance, the clear water that gushes from the heart of the mountain above, as cold almost, as ice." Thus wrote Private Polk to his wife from his lonely solider's vigil in June of 1863.[14]

Colonel Polk, who received a commission as colonel from the General Assembly but chose to enlist and fight as a private, returned home after the war to find his Anson County farm devastated in the wake of Sherman's march. Prior to the war, he had been a gentleman farmer, depending upon the labor of others to provide the sweat and toil for his prosperity.

After the war he had no choice, like thousands of other returning veterans, but to roll up his sleeves and put his own shoulders to the task of rebuilding.

As a member of the General Assembly and as a confidant of Governor Zebulon Vance and other North Carolina leaders, Polk advocated a more progressive method of farming and he fought for the state to take a stronger leadership role in providing research and statistics to help the farmer.

Polk was a natural choice when the Board of Agriculture appointed him as Commissioner of the newly formed Department of Agriculture April 2, 1877, just three weeks before his fortieth birthday.[15]

---

[14] Stuart Noblin, *Leonidas Lafayette Polk: Agrarian Crusader* (Chapel Hill: The University of North Carolina Press, 1949), p. 95.

[15] Ibid, p. 108.

Major responsibilities of the Department were to: compile and distribute statistical and educational information pertaining to agriculture, analyze soil and fertilizer,`restock streams with fish, encourage sheep husbandry, and to foster new industries.[16]

One of the most important jobs of the new department was to test commercial fertilizers and to regulate against fraud and abuse which had become widespread. The use of fertilizer had greatly expanded the acreage available for planting and increased the yield of crops.

Increased demand for fertilizer attracted unscrupulous manufacturers who produced and sold brands that were either inferior or worthless. Polk moved quickly to establish an agriculture laboratory in Chapel Hill where the fertilizers were tested and the results of these tests published. The Department was funded initially by a $500 privilege tax levied upon each manufacturer of fertilizer.

Polk traveled widely throughout the state, meeting with farmers and newspaper editors, promoting progressive farm techniques.

In Asheville, an editor praised his public appearance as, "purely an agriculture speech, intended for the ear of the farmer ... who as head of the Department of Agriculture, we have been fortunate in securing a man not only of great ability but one whose whole heart is in his work."

Another mountain editor wrote of Polk that he was perhaps, "the first man who had ever come from east of the Blue Ridge to address them upon matters of public concern who did not come to seek their votes, and whose personal interest in their immediate welfare did not cease as soon as their votes were deposited in the ballot box." [17]

In March of 1879, the Department of Agriculture published the state's first *Handbook of North Carolina* which contained a large volume of useful information, mostly of agriculture statistics but

---

[16] NC Dept. Of Agriculture, *Report on the Work of the Department of Agriculture,* 1877, Raleigh, NC.

[17] *Asheville Pioneer Republican,* as quoted in the *Farmer and Mechanic,* Sept. 5, 1878.

also of numerous other aspects of farm life. The handbook gave a brief historical sketch of North Carolina from the first days of the colony until 1875. It told about the state's natural resources, railroads, textile mills and the University.

The handbook also gave a brief sketch of each of the counties, including its geographical data, distance from Raleigh, how it was formed, principal products and other useful information. The handbook was such a hit that it was adopted by many schools as a textbook about North Carolina.

The agricultural information in the handbook gave statistics on crops, advised in the use of fertilizer and discussed outstanding achievements in many other aspects of North Carolina farm life, such as fish culture, beekeeping and fruit growing.

After two years of nothing but unqualified praise, the Department began to receive criticism in 1879 for its public expenditures. There was conjecture that Governor Thomas J. Jarvis resented the popularity of Colonel Polk among North Carolina's farmers. Polk also suspected that Kemp Battle, President of the University, envious of the Department's generous funding, worked behind the scenes to persuade the General Assembly to re-organize the Department.

Thus the General Assembly of 1879 divided the Agriculture Department into three equal sub-departments. One was filled by Polk, as Commissioner, another was occupied by the State Geologist and the third by the State Chemist. Polk's monthly reports were abolished and his clerical help dismissed.

Polk resigned as commissioner the following spring and went to work as corresponding editor of the Raleigh News. In 1886 he founded a weekly newspaper devoted to agriculture and called it the *Progressive Farmer*. This publication became the leading farm publication in America and, next to the Bible, was the most read publication for more than half a century. It was published successfully in Raleigh until the 1960s when the company was moved to Birmingham, Alabama, its publisher said at that time to save postage costs. At Birmingham other publishing ventures were begun, including *Southern Living Magazine* and Oxmoor House, a book publishing company. The *Progressive Farmer* companies were sold to Time Warner in the early 1980s for several hundred million dollars.

Polk was active in the move by the Watauga Club to persuade the General Assembly to establish a new college in Raleigh devoted to the study and teaching of agriculture. In spite of the fact that this proposal was ardently opposed by Kemp Battle and other supporters of the University at Chapel Hill who feared the funding for this new school would come from their budget, Polk and the farmers prevailed.

On October 3, 1889 the North Carolina College of Agriculture and Mechanic Arts opened as an agency of the North Carolina Department of Agriculture. That was the humble beginning of North Carolina State University, of which Leonidas Lafayette Polk is remembered as the chief founder. This achievement brought great joy to Polk, for he knew this institution would add greatly to the body of knowledge pertaining to agriculture and related sciences.

Money from the land grant college act of 1862 had been given to the University of North Carolina to be spent on agricultural education; however, not a dime of those funds had been spent to educate a single agriculture student, Polk argued. Using the full power of the influential *Progressive Farmer,* Polk fired a barrage of editorials criticizing the North Carolina General Assembly and threatened to "Elect a legislature that will give it to us." The victory was a particularly sweet one for Polk because it meant a personal loss for Kemp Battle, who Polk believed was the person most responsible for his resignation from the Commissioner's post.

Two years after the opening of State College, Polk led another effort to establish an institution of higher education. That school at Raleigh was "Baptist Female University" and later the name was changed to "Baptist University for Women." Since 1909 it has been called "Meredith College."

Polk continued to play an active role in state and national farm policy until his death in June of 1892. At the time of his death, he was considered the most likely nominee to lead the People's Party as its Presidential candidate.

Montford McGehee

1880-1887

Polk was succeeded by Montford McGehee of Person County, who according to Josephus Daniels was "a classical scholar who had lost three fortunes trying to farm."[18]

The Harvard educated McGehee served as Commissioner until 1887 during a turbulent period, amid much criticism from progressives who rebelled at the conservative management of the Department. Under his caretaker regime, the Department's plan of work essentially continued the tasks begun under the energetic Polk, primarily the publication of the handbook and other statistical reports, the testing of fertilizer, geological surveys, and promotion of fish farming.

Daniels made a thorough study of the Department of Agriculture under McGehee's tutelage and concluded in a full page story in his State Chronicle "...that the Department of Agriculture which ought to be a vital connection between the farmers and the State, was not functioning in a way really to help dirt farmers."

Daniels was unmercifully harsh on the erudite McGehee whose farm had fallen upon hard times during Reconstruction. "He can write more learnedly about agriculture than any man in the State but never made a dollar on his farm."

And then, apparently having second thoughts about his harsh judgment upon this public servant, cooled his rhetoric a bit, writing of McGehee"...though he did not fit in with modern needs, he served with the highest integrity."

John Robinson

1887-1895

John Robinson of Anson County, was elected Commissioner by the Board of Agriculture on April 2, 1887, and served until 1895. He was primarily a caretaker of the office that was divided and weakened by the recent legislative re-organization.

---

[18] Josephus Daniels, *Tar Heel Editor*, (Chapel Hill: The University of North Carolina Press, 1939), p. 296.

Samuel Legerwood Patterson

1895-1897

1899-1908

Samuel Patterson of Caldwell County served as Commissioner of Agriculture from 1895 until 1897 when he was replaced by the Fusionist Party. He was elected by the General Assembly on March 6, 1899, and re-elected by popular vote in 1900 and 1904. He died in office September 14, 1908.

The son of a prominent political family, his father had served in a variety of clerkships in the General Assembly and was State Treasurer from 1835-37.

The younger Patterson represented Yadkin County in the State House in 1891 and 1898 and in the state senate in 1893. In the legislature he was chairman of the Committee on Agriculture.

Patterson Hall at North Carolina State University is named for him.[19]

James M. Mewborne,

1897

James M. Mewborne was elected by the Board of Agriculture on March 23, 1897 to take office June 15, 1897. He served until his resignation effective January 1, 1898.[20]

Mr. Mewborne, of Lenoir County, was a prominent leader of the Farmers' Alliance movement, holding several state and local offices, including State President from 1893 until 1895. He was a liberal Democrat who joined the People's Party (Populist) and was elected to the State Senate in 1895. When the Republicans joined forces with the People's Party in 1894 and 1896, Mewborne benefitted from the Fusionist Movement which gained complete control of the executive, legislative and judicial branches of state government from 1897 to 1899.[21]

---

[19] William S. Powell, *Dictionary of North Carolina Biography*, Vol. 5 (Chapel Hill: University of North Carolina Press, 1995), p. 37.

[20] *Minutes of the Board of Agriculture*, Dec. 14, 1897 (1887-1899), p. 415.

[21] Powell, p. 261.

Upon his resignation as Commissioner of Agriculture, he became Superintendent of the State Penitentiary, a position he held one year, until the Fusionists were thrown out of office. After the collapse of the People's Party, Mr. Mewborne became a Republican and was elected Lenoir County party chairman.

The State Board of Agriculture valued his brief tenure so highly that it passed the following resolution upon his resignation: "That in accepting the resignation of the Hon. J. M. Mewborne as Commissioner of Agriculture, this Board desired to express and place on the record the statement that the administration of the affairs of the Department since Mr. Mewborne became Commissioner has been characterized by honesty, economy and intelligent management. No public officer has ever given more faithful and discriminating attention to the duties of his office than has Mr. Mewborne since he assumed the duties of Commissioner and this Board is confident that the same honesty, economy and intelligent management which he has displayed in the conduct of the affairs of this Department will attend the administration of the affairs of the state in the responsible place which Mr. Mewborne is to fill on and after the first day of January next." [22]

John R. Smith
1897-1899

John R. Smith of Wayne County was elected by the Board of Agriculture on December 14, 1897, to complete the term of Mr. Mewborne.[23]

Mr. Smith came to serve in this high office by the most bizarre set of circumstance of any of the great men who preceded or followed him. He was appointed Superintendent of the State Penitentiary by Republican Governor Russell. An investigation of his tenure there uncovered "considerable squandering and stealing." [24] In his next address to the General Assembly, Governor Russell

---

[22] *Minutes*, Board of Agriculture, p. 429.

[23] Ibid, p. 415.

[24] William S. Powell, *North Carolina Through Four Centuries*, (Chapel Hill: University of North Carolina Press, 1989), p. 435.

noted that the State Penitentiary Accounts were $100,000 short but attributed this to low cotton prices.

Rather than discipline Mr. Smith or have him prosecuted, Governor Daniel L. Russell merely had Smith exchange offices with Commissioner of Agriculture James M. Mewborne. More controversy resulted when it was discovered that neither Mr. Mewborne nor Mr. Smith had made regular reports and discharged other official duties as required by law.

The manner in which Mr. Smith's appointment is recorded is strange, too. When the Board assembled for its regular meeting on December 14, 1897, there is a note in the minutes that Governor Russell wished to speak to the entire Board, so it adjourned to the Governor's office. Following its resumption of business, the matter of Commissioner Mewborne's resignation is duly and sadly noted and a brief sentence announces the appointment of John R. Smith.

At the Board's very next meeting, on June 14, 1898, a motion was made, and apparently hotly debated to "deem the present Commissioner (Mr. Smith) unfitted for that position," and to appoint a committee to request his resignation before the next Board meeting. The motion was tabled.[25]

Samuel L. Patterson
1899-1908

William Alexander Graham
1908-1923

William Alexander Graham of Lincoln County was the son of a prominent North Carolina family, though no kin to my family, as far as I have been able to determine. He was appointed Commissioner of Agriculture September 16, 1908, upon the death in office of Mr. Samuel Patterson. He was subsequently elected to the post until his death December 24, 1923, when he was succeeded by his son. Graham's opponent in his first election campaign was "Farmer Bob" Scott, father of W. Kerr Scott.

Graham had joined the Confederate Army as a second lieutenant and fought in several battles until he was wounded at

---

[25] *Minutes*, Board of Agriculture, p. 443.

Gettysburg. After the war he returned to his grandfather's plantation in Lincoln County and became a farmer. During the difficult Reconstruction years, he worked hard and improved the productivity of the farm with shrewd management and by using the latest improvements at his disposal.

Mr. Graham was an active supporter of the Farmer's Alliance, serving as state president in 1901, 1902 and 1905. He is credited with developing the North Carolina Alliance's business agency which became a unique innovation in the United States.

He was elected to the State Senate in 1878 and to the North Carolina House of Representatives in 1905. In the State Legislature, he gained a well-deserved reputation as being an outspoken friend of the farmer and a supporter of progressive agriculture. This led to his appointment in 1899 to the Board of Agriculture where he served until his election in 1908 as Commissioner of Agriculture.

Mr. Graham is remembered for his persistent inquiry into the decline of agriculture during the early 1900s. His findings -- poor soil, poor farming methods, poor machinery, poor crop strains and poor animal stock -- led to a better understanding of the causes of poor productivity of the typical North Carolina farm in his day and the growing dependence upon imported food.

As commissioner, he established laboratories and experimental stations to study and improve soil conditions and to develop new varieties of seed and new treatments for orchards and truck gardens. He organized farmers' institutes where demonstrations of improved farming methods, machinery and home improvement helped farmers elevate their productivity.

Within a decade, Mr. Graham's scholarly and scientific approach to the great farming problems of his day resulted in significant improvement of soil, livestock, farm machinery and farm methods. His leadership and vision resulted in a vast change for the better for the average farmer and for North Carolina.

William Alexander Graham, Jr.

1923-1936

Upon the death of his father, William Alexander Graham, Jr. was appointed Commissioner of Agriculture in 1923 and he held his post until defeated for re-election in 1936 by William Kerr Scott. He was primarily a caretaker of the office, continuing the many innovations that his father had initiated but not taking any bold steps of his own.

This was an unfortunate time for timid leadership. It was the peak of the Great Depression. Not only were farm prices depressed--cotton had sunk again to a nickel a pound and pork to less than four cents a pound--but there was also a resurgence in animal disease and crop pests. Hog cholera was rampant and the boll weevil devastated cotton fields.

North Carolina farmers yearned for new leadership in 1936 and Mr. Graham became the only incumbent Commissioner of Agriculture to be defeated for re-election.

He served three terms in the North Carolina Senate, first in 1923 and later in 1939 and 1943.

William Kerr Scott
1936-1949

W. Kerr Scott, a future Governor and future U.S. Senator first ran for public office in 1936, challenging incumbent Commissioner of Agriculture William A. Graham. Scott, the accomplished and progressive Extension Agent of Alamance County, defeated Graham in the Democratic Primary by 20,000 votes and served three terms as Commissioner. One of his major achievements was leading the successful effort to rid the state of Bang's disease, a cattle ailment.

Two years after his election as Commissioner, the *Progressive Farmer* chose Scott as its "Man of the Year" for the dramatic way he had energized the Department. During the 12 years he served in that post, Scott accumulated a strong political base among the state's farmers who appreciated what he had done for them.

A story from his early life illustrates his commitment to agriculture even as a young man. In 1917, the young Scott was sent to New Hanover County to speak to a group of farm youth, encouraging them to produce heartily for the war effort.

He exhorted them to do their share by working hard and growing the essential food for the troops. "One bushel of potatoes is equivalent to 200 bullets shot at the enemy," Scott later recalled his remarks. The next morning, he went down to the Army recruitment office in Wilmington and enlisted, serving during World War I in the field artillery.[26]

He resigned his office in 1948 and announced his campaign for Governor, challenging the powerful "Shelby Dynasty" which had dominated the North Carolina Democratic Party for more than 20 years. Scott promised that if elected he would get North Carolina farmers out of the mud by building a network of farm to market roads throughout the state. He placed second in the first primary out of a field of six candidates. During a second primary run-off election, Scott defeated incumbent Treasurer Charles M. Johnson, who had been favored, and easily won the November general election. Scott became the first farmer elected Governor of North Carolina in the 20th Century.

As Commissioner, Scott energized the office and used the full weight of state government bureaucracy to improve the quality of seed, fertilizer and livestock feed. He reported of his first two years' work: "It was discovered, early in my administration that a large percent of feed contained worthless filler materials such as rice hulls, oat hulls, corn stalk, wheat straw and other similar materials having little or no feed value.

"By and large, our farmers can now buy feed with the assurance that it is equal to the guaranteed analysis, the ingredients claimed are present and if labeled a 'special purpose feed,' it will be suitable for that purpose. False and misleading labeling of feed is not tolerated."

Other achievements during the Scott years included the state taking over operation of the North Carolina State Fair in 1937, expansion of the test farm operations, beefing up the marketing division and increasing the work of the statistical division so that its output was relevant and helpful to the working farmer.

At the end of his 12 years as Commissioner, Mr. Scott made a speech to a joint meeting of the North Carolina Cotton Growers'

---

[26] Press Release, NC Dept.of Agriculture, Nov. 4, 1939, by Louis H. Wilson (NC Archives, Dept. Of Agriculture Records, Commissioner's Office), Box 22.

Cooperative and the North Carolina Farm Cooperative Exchange in Raleigh which included an impressive audience of some 5,000 farm supporters.

In that speech he summed up the philosophy he had developed as he championed the interest of North Carolina's rural farm constituency and it became the theme upon which he built his successful campaign for Governor. Here is the essence of that speech in a tightly written summary, "With a farm income on par with the rest of society, with good health facilities, good roads, electricity, telephones, a revived country church program and improved rural schools--with these firmly fixed in our rural life, we can stand as a bulwark against the breakdowns that may occur in our state economy or its moral structure.

On this rock let us build."[27]

His most significant agriculture achievement came during his term as Governor when he kept his promise to build a system of farm-to-market roads across North Carolina that led directly to the beginning of the state's most prosperous era of agriculture.

David S. Coltrane

1948-1949

David S. Coltrane, of Wake County, was appointed by Governor Cherry on February 14, 1948, to replace W. Kerr Scott who resigned to run for Governor. He had been an able assistant to Commissioner Scott who credited Mr. Coltrane with doing the behind the scenes work that resulted in vast improvement in the quality of seed, fertilizer and feed sold to North Carolina farmers.

Lynton Yates Ballentine

1949-1964

L.Y. Ballentine served as Lieutenant Governor from 1945-1949 and had aspirations to become Governor. However, his Democratic friends among the "Shelby Dynasty" preferred State Treasurer Charles Johnson who was defeated by incumbent

---

[27] Speech to the NC Cotton Growers' Cooperative and NC Farm Cooperative Exchange, Raleigh, NC Sept. 30, 1947, (NC Dept. Of Agriculture Records, Commissioner's Office, NC Archives), Box 22.

Commissioner of Agriculture W. Kerr Scott for the Democratic nomination for Governor.

Mr. Ballentine, a Wake County dairy farmer, wisely chose to fall back to his preferred profession and became a very good steward of North Carolina's good land during the final, productive years of his life. Just before he died, he wrote the foreword to the last North Carolina Agricultural Statistics report, beginning with his favorite Biblical quotation, "You shall know the truth and the truth shall make you free."

He went on to explain that agriculture is a complex business venture and its continued growth and survival calls for maximum efficiency in operation and planning. Basic current and historic facts about agricultural production are essential to good planning and management of farming operations. Farmers and agricultural workers must, therefore, be kept fully informed and up-to-date in their knowledge of developments in production and marketing.

Mr. Ballentine was extremely proud of the fact that the farmer had made so much progress in the century in which he lived. He noted in the 1960 Statistical Report that in 1850 the U.S. farmer produced enough food for himself and three other people and that by his time the farmer produced food for himself and 25 other people.

Mr. Ballentine held a number of important regional and national positions which were testament to his great character. Among them, trustee of his alma mater, Wake Forest University; Vice President of the National Association of State Departments of Agriculture and Chairman of the United States Department of Agriculture Marketing Committee. He served as a member of the Wake Board of Commissioners and represented Wake County in the North Carolina State Senate. During his tenure as Lieutenant Governor, he also served as Chairman of the State Board of Education.

Mr. Ballentine died in office July 19, 1964.

James Allen Graham

Born April 7, 1921 in Cleveland, NC (Rowan County) to James Turner and Laura Allen Graham.
Elementary and High School education in Cleveland Schools.
B.S. in Agriculture, NC State University, 1942.

1942-45	Agriculture teacher, Iredell County
1946-52	Superintendent, Upper Mountain Research Station, Laurel Springs, NC
1952-55	Manager, Winston-Salem Fair (now the Dixie Classic)
1955-56	Secretary, N. C. Herford Association
1956-64	General Manager, Raleigh Farmers Market
1964-	Appointed July 30 to fill unexpired term of L.Y. Ballentine, as North Carolina Commissioner of Agriculture by Governor Terry Sanford
1964-	Elected in general election and re-elected very four years since.

During his tenure as the longest serving Commissioner of Agriculture in the United States, Jim Graham has served as president of the National Association of State Departments of Agriculture (NASDA), president of the Southern Association of State Departments of Agriculture (SASDA) and president of the Southern United States Trade Association (SUSTA).

He is an active Kiwanian and past president of the Raleigh Kiwanis Club, a Shriner: a deacon in the First Baptist Church of Raleigh; has served on the Boards of the Raleigh Rescue Mission, N. C. Society to Prevent Blindness and Campbell University. He is permanent class president of the Class of 1942 at NCSU; and a former trustee at N. C. A&T State University.

He is married to the former Helen Kirk, and they have two daughters, Mrs. Alice G. Underhill of New Bern, N.C. and Connie G. Brooks of Nashville, Tennessee. He has six grandchildren.

Jim Graham, is the recipient of numerous awards and honors from local, state and national commodity organizations, educational institutions, banks, civic and farmer groups for his unselfish and dedicated service to agriculture.

Chapter 4

North Carolina Department of Agriculture

"Agriculture not only gives riches to the nation, but the only riches she can call her own." Samuel Johnston

The role of the North Carolina Department of Agriculture and the scope of its work has increased dramatically since that humble beginning in 1877 when the Department was established, largely to protect farmers from the greed of unscrupulous fertilizer dealers.

Today, the department's some 1,500 employees work within 17 divisions toward the important goal of promoting and protecting a steady supply of food and fiber in North Carolina. Our mission has never changed; however, the scope of our work and the variety of challenges we face on a day to day basis have changed immensely.

The most conspicuous tasks we perform involve the things we do to help the farmer produce a better product, protect it from disease and insects and market those products to a constantly growing and changing consumer population. Also, the Department enforces many rules and regulations based on the some 50 laws and special programs enacted by the General Assembly to protect the health, safety and welfare of North Carolina citizens.

Aquaculture

Aquaculture, or fish farming, is a relatively new industry in the state and one that promises steady growth. Fin fish and shellfish are now routinely raised in man-made ponds and cages. The demand for fish has grown in recent years, the result of greater awareness of fish as a healthy source of protein.

North Carolina farmers raise trout, catfish, hybrid striped bass, clams and crawfish. Trout are raised in the mountains. Catfish, crawfish and hybrid striped bass farms are found mostly in the eastern part of the state. Clam production is concentrated at the coast.

Fish farming has a great potential for expanding farm income in North Carolina and offers yet another opportunity for diversification.

Agronomic Services

Agronomy is the science of growing crops and managing soil. This process has changed vastly since the first English colonists were taught primitive planting techniques by the native Americans. The Agronomic Division's state-of-the-art, automated laboratory analyzes soil, plant tissue, water and animal wastes for levels of plant nutrients, heavy metals and other agriculturally relevant elements. It also assays soil samples for populations of plant-parasitic nematodes. These services form the basis for effective fertilizer, lime and crop management recommendations.

The Division's scientifically based recommendations help optimize crop yields and beautify yards throughout the state as well as minimize water pollution. By following the guidelines in their agronomic reports, growers both maximize profit and protect the environment by applying no more lime, fertilizer and other production inputs than necessary. As a result, movement of fertilizer nitrates, phosphates and nematicides into ground and surface water is reduced.

A statewide network of field advisory specialists is available to provide grower assistance. Known as regional agronomists, these specialists help growers identify and solve plant nutrient problems and interpret and implement recommended practices in the most cost effective and environmentally safe way. As an additional avenue of outreach, Division reports and publications are available online via the Internet.

The Agronomic Division is known internationally for the soil testing methodologies it has developed. These methods are based on decades of research, field observation and laboratory verification. Soil nutrient extractants developed by Dr. Adolph Mehlich, former consultant to the Division, have proven to be accurate for soils with a wide range of physical and chemical properties. As a result, these extractants are now used routinely by soil testing laboratories throughout the world. Scientists from 67 countries have attended training sessions at the North Carolina facility.

Demand for Division services and the ability to meet that demand has increased dramatically since testing began in 1939. The volume of samples analyzed each year has more than quadrupled to 300,000. This trend is expected to continue as long as agricultural productivity and environmental quality are established statewide goals.

Our agronomy laboratory has achieved worldwide acclaim for the quality of work done. Representatives from all over this country and from nearly 70 foreign countries have visited the laboratory and observed our activities.

Food and Drug Protection

The primary mission of the Food and Drug Protection Division is to administer the North Carolina laws that assure foods, animal feeds, drugs and medical devices, cosmetics, pesticides, and automotive antifreezes are safe, wholesome, unadulterated, properly labeled, registered, manufactured, stored and distributed in a manner that guarantees the safety of the product to the consumer and to the environment.

This Division is one of the unsung heroes of the North Carolina Department of Agriculture. Its work is vitally important to the citizens of North Carolina. And yet, the men and women who perform this extremely valuable service for their fellow citizens seldom get the credit they deserve.

Food and Drug Protection Division inspectors routinely inspect food and drug processors and distributors. They observe raw materials being received from dairymen, fishermen, cattlemen, and all farmers who produce the good foods we enjoy and depend upon for our sustenance. Vehicles which transport foods are inspected to make sure that the products are kept at the proper temperatures and that no foreign materials contaminate the products as they are moved. Storage facilities are inspected to assure that they are free of rodents, insects and other pests and that storage conditions are proper to prevent contamination from other sources. During a typical year, the Division's inspectors will conduct approximately 9,000 inspections, each of which is designed to protect the consumer.

Samples are taken routinely during inspections at many points along the production, processing and distribution chain. Laboratory tests are conducted to detect problems that are likely to affect a specific type of food as it moves through distribution toward the family table. For example, fresh fruits and vegetables are tested for pesticides that might have been applied in the field to control insects, weeds or other unwanted pests. If a product is found to be contaminated, impure or mislabeled, prompt action is taken to protect the public from harm. Embargoes may be imposed and the food product destroyed.

Raw milk, fresh from the farm, is checked for pesticide residues and for natural toxins that can occur in livestock feeds. Once the milk reaches the processing plant, more tests are conducted to ensure that bacteria levels are within an acceptable range and that no disease organisms are present after processing. If the milk is used to make ice cream, cheese, butter or other products, more samples are taken to assure that these products contain safe ingredients.

Inspectors also respond to a wide range of consumer complaints from foreign objects in packaged products to food-borne illnesses.

Pesticides are registered with the Division's Pesticide Section. Pesticide applicators are licensed to make sure they use pesticides properly. Pesticide samples are collected to check for proper labeling and to test the levels of active ingredients. The pesticide laboratory conducts about 3,500 soil sample tests each year.

Chemists within the Division analyze food and drug samples, animal feeds, pesticides, cosmetics and automotive antifreezes to make sure consumers are buying clean, safe and wholesome products. Tests are made for unlawful or harmful additives, toxic substances or bacterial contamination, and to ensure products are properly labeled.

The Division performs its work to an extremely high standard. Computerized testing has replaced many test tube methods which results in more exact measurement. For example, the term "parts per billion" is used routinely to refer to chemical test results. A "part per billion" is equal to one inch in 16,000 miles, or one pinch of salt in ten tons of potato chips. Now our scientists are beginning to test for pollutants and impurities in the micro-minute quantities of "parts per trillion." Precise determinations of chemical findings are crucial to maintaining a healthy food supply.

During a normal year, the feed laboratory will conduct tests on some 5,000 commercial feed samples and 3,000 farm forage samples. In 1995, there were 67 stop sale orders issued and 225 non-registered commercial feeds were found in the market place. The fertilizer laboratory will also test about 10,000 fertilizer and lime samples each year.

A few years ago this Division, along with the Sate Health Department, became involved in an international episode which clearly demonstrated the high quality of their work. The laboratory attempted to use a popular brand of bottled water, which it thought to be pure, as a standard to which it could compare other test results. Scientists tested the product samples in question and found them to contain impurities to the extent of 17 parts per billion.

Robert Gordon, pharmacist and our very able director of the Food and Drug Division, contacted the U.S. Food and Drug Administration who in turn notified the U.S. State Department and told them of the problem. We were advised by the State Department to ignore the problem because the manufacturer of this product was a giant in its field with very deep pockets. We were told quite bluntly that this big foreign firm would not stand for the State of North Carolina to mess with its reputation.

Against the recommendation of the federal folks, we issued a press release disclosing the problem with the product. Instead of challenging our finding, they ran their own tests and admitted the problem. Their solution to the problem was to change the label for the product, which they did to our satisfaction.

After the crisis was over, their scientists compared notes with ours and found that the results of their tests were identical to ours. By their own account, their product was 17 parts per billion short of being pure. I was proud of our people in this highly visible situation. This was not an unusual situation and happens quite often.

Great care is taken to make sure that the food is safe from the farm to the kitchen table. It is important that the consumer have confidence in the products which are purchased for the family to eat and use.

Our constant vigilance means much to North Carolina consumers. First, we must identify problems before they become a crisis and solve them at an early stage. More than that, our reputation as an aggressive and competent protection agency deters many unscrupulous merchants from trying to peddle inferior products in North Carolina. They know we will find them and stop them. I have heard from my counterparts in other states with more lax consumer product laws about incidents where they found shoddy products that were not even distributed in North Carolina.

I am confident that the work of this Division is as good as that of any other program of its type in the country. It is superior to most other programs. This Division has received several national honors in recognition of its outstanding work. My greatest reward, however, is to know that the people of North Carolina enjoy safe food and other products as the result of our stewardship.

Food Distribution

Millions of dollars worth of USDA commodities are served to North Carolina's 1.1 million public school children each year. This wholesome food is provided by the North Carolina Department of Agriculture Food Distribution Division. Public school cafeterias are a major recipient of food from the U.S. Department of Agriculture commodity food program. Other recipients include soup kitchens, food banks, emergency feeding organizations, the elderly and other public institutions such as prisons.

Foods distributed under this program include frozen and canned meats and vegetables, peanut butter, fruit juices, flour, canned fruit and cheese. This program provides an important source of appetizing and nutritious food to a deserving constituency. Its purchase by the federal government stabilizes prices for critical foodstuffs and offers basic economic security to the participating farmers.

Each year the Food Distribution Division delivers some $30 million in donated commodities from the U. S. Department of Agriculture to nine different local, state and federal programs which include 632 different agencies. Of this total, about $23 million in commodities go to public and private schools for use in the Food and Nutrition Program.

Marketing

Promoting North Carolina's agricultural products is a major duty of the Department and this job is performed by the Marketing Division which assists farmers with marketing through traditional channels and new opportunities are being explored continuously.

Recent successful marketing and promotion programs include "Goodness Grows in North Carolina" and "Flavors of Carolina." A "Goodness Grows" logo certifies that the product is homegrown and encourages Tar Heels to consume locally grown foodstuffs. Flavors is a food show for grocery store and restaurant food buyers designed to give them an opportunity to taste North Carolina produced and processed foodstuffs.

The market news section provides up-to-date information about farm prices to newspapers, radio and television stations. This section was the Department's original marketing initiative and paved the way to today's modern, complex marketing strategies.

Farmers' markets are operated in four North Carolina cities: Asheville, the Triad (Greensboro, High Point and Winston-Salem), Charlotte and Raleigh. In these modern market places, farmers display and sell their produce to thousands of urban dwellers who have come to depend upon these outlets for fresh fruits and vegetables, flowers, pumpkins, firewood and other farm products.

The grading and regulatory section where inspectors grade meat and eggs according to freshness is also a part of marketing.

See Chapter 5 for a more detailed discussion of marketing.

Plant Industry

The Plant Industry Division tests seeds for germination and freedom from contamination by other seeds; tests fertilizers for conformity to indicated analysis and monitors insects, plant diseases and weeds. The work of this Division is vitally important to the success of agriculture in North Carolina. As a result of the efforts of this Division, North Carolina farmers can depend upon quality seed to plant their crops, quality fertilizer to grow their crops and an agricultural environment that is vigorously protected from exotic pests organisms in which to grow productive crops. One of the great success stories in the history of North Carolina agriculture is the eradication of the boll weevil and how North Carolina decided to proceed with a program to eradicate this pest despite some "experts" who said it could not be done. We successfully eradicated the boll weevil from northeastern North Carolina between 1978 and 1980. We did it in three years and are now the envy of all cotton producing areas infested by the boll weevil in both North and South America.

The Seed Section of the Plant Industry Division provides oversight of seed products offered for sale in North Carolina by seed label review and sampling and testing by regulatory specialists. Service testing for seed quality is provided to seed producers, farmers, and seedsmen. These quality evaluations include germination potential and identification of noxious weed seed and other contaminants. Seed inspectors check some 24,000 seed lots each year to make sure that growers are getting quality, properly labeled seeds. When substandard seeds are found, a "stop sale" is ordered and the seeds are removed from trade.

More than 150,000 tons of fertilizer are sampled each year to assure that farmers are getting the specified ingredients which they pay for. The program, combined with responsible commercial firms, provides high quality, accurately labeled and competitively priced fertilizer to North Carolina farmers. In the early days of the Department, misrepresented fertilizer was a major problem for North Carolina farmers and, as noted in Chapter 2, such problems were a significant reason for establishing the North Carolina Department of Agriculture.

Plant Pests

Plant specialists work closely with growers to help control and, in some cases, eradicate insects and other plant pests which, if left uncontested, would continue to destroy many crops, as they have done in the past. In 1989, Africanized "killer" bees were found on a freighter in Morehead City. The Department's specialists found the harmful pests and quickly destroyed them. Bee inspectors service more than 16,000 North Carolina beekeepers, routinely checking hives for mites, bee diseases and other problems. In addition to producing delectable honey, bees play an important role in pollinating fruits and vegetables.

The Boll Weevil

"Boll weevil say to de farmer,
You better lemme alone,
I've et up all you' cotton
An' now I'll begin on de co'n!"
From The Ballad

The boll weevil, memorialized in a popular ballad that attests to the mighty power of this persistent pest with its capacious appetite big enough to devour a cotton field, destroyed the cotton crop of the entire South several times. The role of the North Carolina Department of Agriculture in the demise of the boll weevil is one of the Department's great success stories.

In the mid-1970s we began two very significant uphill battles during my tenure as Commissioner of Agriculture, the first being to eradicate hog cholera. The second was the eradication of the cotton boll weevil.

I was surprised by the response of certain authorities to our announced campaign to eradicate the boll weevil. The apathy of pesticide manufacturers who were benefitting immensely from the 10 treatments of infected fields was understandable. However, still to this day I cannot understand the reluctance of certain agricultural scientists, some at that time employed by our own great NC State University who argued against such an effort. They said such an initiative was impossible and had no chance of succeeding. There was even a suggestion that it was wrong to attempt to eliminate a species, even a species as harmful as the boll weevil, a bad little bug which possesses no good attributes as far as I know.

The boll weevil (Anthonomus grandis) was once the most serious cotton pest in North America and still is a major problem in several other southern states, mainly Texas and Mississippi. The tiny little insect averages no more than a quarter inch in length but packs a terrific wallop. It has been estimated that the boll weevil still destroys as many as 5 million bales of cotton annually in North and South America, which at today's prices would place the loss at some $20 billion.

It is believed the boll weevil came to the United States in about 1890 from Mexico.

In the spring, after emerging from overwintering quarters, the adult female boll weevil lays from 100 to 300 eggs, carefully depositing each of them in cotton buds. The weevils are respectful of each other, careful not to lay an egg in a bud which has been visited already by another female. That social consideration results in almost total devastation of each infested cotton field. Within two to three weeks from the time the egg is laid, it hatches and matures into an adult boll weevil. Because of such a short gestation period, ten new generations of boll weevils can emerge in a single year.

The larvae live entirely in the cotton fruit, consuming and destroying the seed and surrounding fiber. Because they reside inside the cotton bolls for their entire period of development they are beyond the influence of pesticides. By the time a new adult emerges from his adolescent home which has been destroyed, he is ready to start a new family in another cotton bud and repeat the process.

Left unchallenged the boll weevil is the most awesome foe of the cotton farmer. That is why we took on this pest and vowed to eradicate him. It was clear that if we did not eradicate the boll weevil, the boll weevil would eradicate the cotton farmer.

North Carolina's boll weevil campaign began in the mid-1970s. Marshall Grant, a Garysburg, North Carolina farmer was a leading supporter of the initiative. Howard Singletary of my staff who is now the Director of the Plant Division, also played a major role. Bill Dickerson, now Plant Pest Administrator for the Department, was a key scientist who developed improved trapping technology for this program.

A three-year plan was developed for a trial boll weevil program on some 30,000 acres in northeastern North Carolina. The experimental program consisted of a comprehensive program of survey and treatment. The survey using pheromone traps allowed the program to treat only those cotton fields infested with boll weevils. This greatly reduced the amount of insecticide needed to eradicate the weevil. The bright, colorful boll weevil traps became a popular landmark in cotton fields during this period.

The traps consisted of a capture cylinder on top of a funnel attached to a one quarter plastic cup painted lime green, a shocking color to humans but one that is especially appealing to boll weevils. The key element of the trap is synthetic pheromone, a powerful attractant that boll weevils use to find each other. The weevils are attracted both by the green color of the trap and the pheromone. This combination of attractants allow the trap to detect a single boll weevil in a cotton field.

Funding for the program was shared equally among farmers and the government. Twenty-five percent of the fund was provided by the State of North Carolina, 25 percent by the federal government and 50 percent by farmers. Total cost of the treatment program averaged about $75 per acre, an amount far less than the estimated benefits of the program each year. Obviously, this was money well spent.

The boll weevil was eradicated from the remainder of North Carolina between 1983 and 1987. As a result of this successful program, farmers reduced the number of insecticide treatments by 75 percent. Cotton acreage in North Carolina has increased 20-fold since the boll weevil was eradicated.

We still continue an aggressive boll weevil monitoring program in North Carolina. This program is managed by employees of the Plant Industry Division. In 1997, growers paid $3.60 an acre to keep the weevils out of North Carolina. Although we have solved our boll weevil problem, the highly migratory pest still exists in other southern states and from time to time, a few isolated insects make their way here. Some may hitchhike on used cotton equipment; others may be brought in by vistors in an automobile or truck.

A total of 721,000 acres of cotton was planted in North Carolina in 1996. Cotton was grown in 63 of the state's 100 counties in 1996 compared to only 13 counties in 1978. Nearly 120,000 boll weevil traps were installed in some 60,000 fields. Weevils were discovered in only two North Carolina cotton fields in 1996. They were carefully treated and eradicated. North Carolina had fewer than 300 cotton farmers in 1978 when the eradication program started. That number had increased to 4,500 in 1996. Since the boll weevil was eradicated from this state in 1987 fewer than 200 acres of cotton have been treated for boll weevil while we've produced more than 3.5 million acres of cotton.

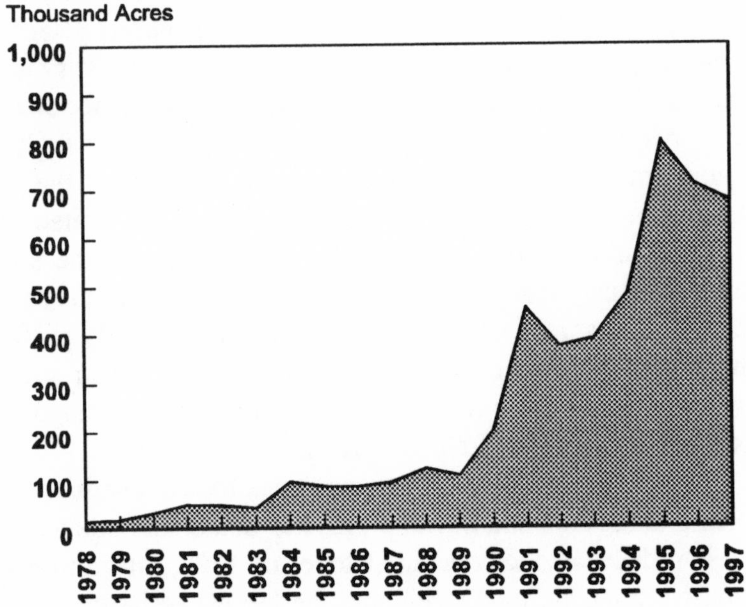

Cotton Acreage Planted in North Carolina 1978-1997
Table 5

Gypsy Moth

Similar pest control methods, including intensive monitoring with pheromone traps, are being used to control and destroy gypsy moths. The gypsy moth was accidently released in Massachusetts in 1869 and has since spread to northeastern North Carolina. This pest eats leaves of our trees, especially hardwoods and will wipe out an entire forest in a few years.

Since 1972, the Department in cooperation with other agencies has made aerial and/or ground treatments to more than 100,000 acres of forestland in more than 110 locations across the state to control the gypsy moth. In many instances the gypsy moth was eradicated as a direct result of the treatment. The overall result has been the containment and control of the spread of the gypsy moth in North Carolina. The entire state is surveyed to detect the presence of gypsy moth. In 1996, some 31,000 gypsy moth traps were placed across the state and 13,534 moths were captured.

In July of 1993, a container ship, USCS Advantage, traveling from Nordenham, Germany, docked at Military Ocean Terminal, Sunny Point, N.C. Subsequent inspections determined that the ship was infested with a mixed strain of gypsy moths containing DNA heritage of both the Asian and European gypsy moths. Along with the DNA heritage the capacity for flight was observed among the female gypsy moths. Females of the gypsy moths known to occur in the northeastern part of the United States and Canada do not fly. The moths swarmed from the ship to Brunswick County trees. Since female Asian gypsy moths can fly, wide and rapid spread of the pest was considered highly probable. Without control measures, the newly introduced Asian strain of gypsy moth would likely render millions of dollars of damage to the forests and landscapes of North Carolina.

The Department and other agencies took immediate action to form a task force and develop plans to detect and eradicate this newly introduced exotic pest. In October of 1996, after three years of intensive trapping, monitoring and the largest aerial treatment of an exotic insect pest ever to take place in the Untied States, the Asian gypsy moth was declared eradicated from North Carolina. The Plant Industry Division was the lead agency involved with every aspect of this challenging and successful project to rid North Carolina of another highly destructive insect pest.

The Department also monitors the population of other pest insects such as fire ants and sweet potato weevils and conducts

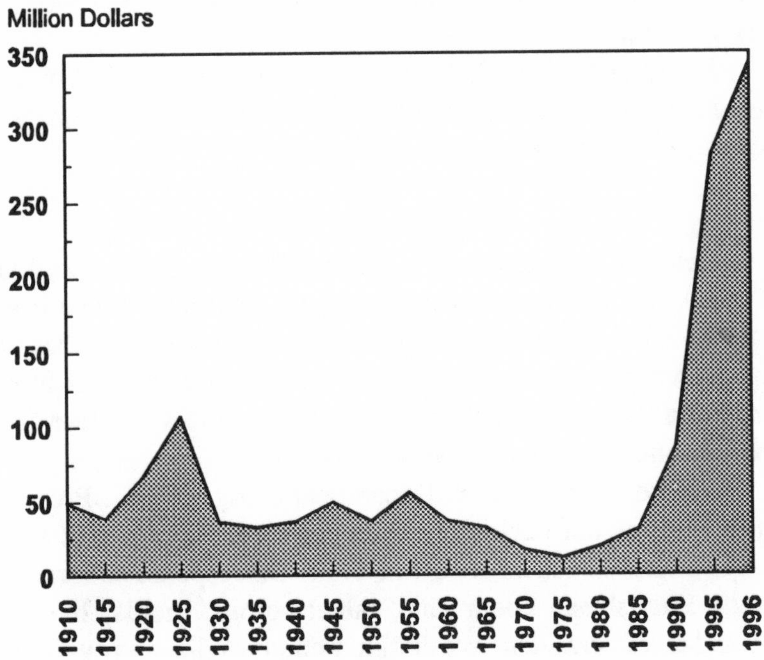

Value of North Carolina Cotton Production, 1910-1996
Table 6

programs to reduce the impact of these and other pests. Programs to survey, monitor, control and eradicate noxious weeds such as purple loosestrife, witchweed, tropical soda apple, itchgrass and clover broomrape are in place and continue to be successful.

Other Duties

It is the duty of the Department through the Plant Industry Division to protect endangered plants that are threatened with extinction such as Venus' flytrap. The natural habitat of this plant is limited to a 75-mile radius of Wilmington and is constantly being reduced by development. Ginseng, which grows naturally in the mountains of Western North Carolina, is endangered because the high demand for extracts from this plant in Asia where it is believed to possess strong medicinal powers.

In 1996 seed inspectors checked seeds at some 3,200 licensed retail and wholesale seed dealers. A total of 3,405 official seed samples were collected from 24,509 seed lots and 527 stop sale orders were issued.

Penalties totaling $533,244 were assessed on 292,769 tons of fertilizer and lime. One hundred twenty-two stop sales were issued on fertilizer and lime lot violations.

Statistics

Collecting and reporting statistics about crops produced and sold was a major function of the original Department when it was created in 1877. Until that time, farmers had no idea what was being grown and what was being sold except for word of mouth information they could pick up from acquaintances or glean from infrequent and occasional news reports.

According to the U. S. Department of Agriculture, President George Washington personally compiled what is regarded as the first agricultural statistical report in 1791. In response to a request from an Englishman about land values, crops, yields, livestock prices and taxes, President Washington conducted a survey himself and developed "the nation's first crop report."

In 1796, Washington proposed the establishment of a National Board of Agriculture and the parsimonious Congress rejected the idea.

In 1839, the Commissioner of Patents persuaded Congress to appropriate $1,000 for "collecting and distributing seeds, carrying out agricultural investigations, and procuring agricultural statistics."

Abraham Lincoln established the U.S. Department of Agriculture in 1862, calling it "the people's department." Its first crop report appeared in July of 1863 and the availability of accurate crop and livestock statistics is said to have helped both northern farmers and the Army of the North during the Civil War.

The Statistics Division of the North Carolina Department of Agriculture continues to this day to perform a vital role in keeping North Carolina farmers informed. When a farmer knows what crops are being grown or how many hogs are being raised, he can make a better decision on what to raise next year.

Analysts transform the statistics into projections, trends, and interpretation of the trends' economic implications. This information is invaluable data to farmers, agribusiness managers, farm lenders and farm policy makers.

The North Carolina Agricultural Statistics division is a joint venture, originating in 1919, between the North Carolina Department of Agriculture and the United States Department of Agriculture's National Agricultural Statistics Service. Nearly 400 reports are issued annually covering most all facets of agriculture, including crops, fruits and vegetables, livestock, dairy, poultry, prices, farm labor, weather-crop reports, cash receipts, aquaculture, and other items of interest. State and county estimates are published for major commodities.

Research Stations

Eighteen research stations across the state experiment with different ways to grow plants and animals. The purpose of these experiments is to find better ways to grow improved crops more efficiently and better ways to raise healthier livestock. These research stations are a joint venture between the North Carolina Department of Agriculture and North Carolina State University.

Research benefits both farmers and consumers through the great abundance, high quality, and low price of American food and fiber produced by a very small percentage of our population. The primary focus of the Division of Research Stations and State Farms is to support and encourage agricultural research as well as disseminate results in development of new plant and fruit varieties, the study of variables affecting plant (soils, fertilizer, chemicals, pests, and diseases) innovations in livestock production and management, development in the technology of equipment, conservation and environmental schemes, and other similar areas.

Research programs must deal with the complex interrelationships of cultural practices, adaptability, and control of insects, diseases, weeds and other pests in a way to give maximum yield with minimal damage to people and the environment.

In order to apply laboratory research findings in field situations, the North Carolina Department of Agriculture and North Carolina Agricultural Research Service developed a system of 15 outlying research stations and three state farms. These varied locations provide unique production belts, soil types, and environments to allow research of issues and problems unique to specific locations. Many of today's successful production practices have resulted from research conducted at these branch stations.

How Does Research Help the Farmer?

Research projects include work with field and forage crops, Christmas trees, burley tobacco, poultry and livestock, which includes beef cattle, sheep, and goats. Breeding studies are conducted for increased yield, quality, drought and disease resistance for field and horticultural crops.

Pest management, and studies of insects, diseases and weeds provide information for improved pest control. Soil related pests applied research is conducted in the areas of physiology, environmental influences, control and eradication procedures, and application methodology.

Genetic engineering of plant materials offers the hope of increased yields; improved resistance to disease and insects; reduction in the use of pesticides; enhanced nutritional quality and flavor; and improved product storage, shipping and processing traits. Studies involving genetics and engineering are currently being performed with corn, cotton, tobacco, soybeans, and various horticultural crops.

Biotechnical research using fungi, nematodes, beneficial insects and gene splicing is increasingly prevalent in the search for environmentally safe disease and pest management practices. The use of biological materials such as beneficial insects and genetic engineering to control disease and insects reduces the amount of chemical inputs into the environment. The application of this technology is evaluated to determine if it can be integrated safely and effectively into vegetable production.

New and improved chemistry requires the continuous testing of insecticides, herbicides, fungicides and growth regulators to determine the effectiveness and safety of chemical compounds in the production of agricultural commodities.

Plant physiology studies focus on environmental and physiological factors affecting plant growth and development. The growth and development of a plant is determined by genetic makeup, environmental conditions and cultural practices.

Cultural evaluation studies help find better ways to utilize and track nutrients applied to crops. Research is directed toward learning the amount of nutrients to apply, when to apply them, and how these nutrients move through the soil profile.

Research is conducted to answer questions on environmental concerns and sustainable agriculture technology. Studies are carried out to monitor fertilizers and pesticides as they move through the soil or leave the field in run-off water. Also, conservation studies are conducted to reduce soil tillage, as well as pesticide and fertilizer use.

Research is conducted to look for alternative crops such as herbs, spices, garlic, mushrooms and ginseng. Cultural techniques have been developed for these crops. The search for Integrated Pest Management on these crops and methods of organically growing them continue.

Studies are being conducted to find better and more efficient ways to produce native ornamental plants such as rhododendron, azalea and mountain laurel. Techniques for growing from seed and cuttings are being developed. Studies of the effect of cultural practices from the plant bed to the salable plant are being conducted to assure the industry and consumer a plant with a high survival index. Urban growing conditions can vary from ideal to severe and attention is given to the development of plants that will tolerate the entire range.

Cold water fish, particularly trout, are an important part of North Carolina's economy. Research efforts concentrate on solving production problems and developing new techniques such as water recycling and filtration for maximum utilization of water resources to produce fish for food. Feed conversion is being studied to give better feed to weight grain ratios. Techniques to reduce the nutrient content of discharge water from fish operations are getting a closer look.

The emphasis of composting research is on production of a high quality product from such diverse things as municipal garbage, agricultural waste, forest waste and animal and fish carcasses. Co-composting the other materials with sewage sludge is also part of the studies. The products of the composting are tested for their use as a soil amendment and growing medium for greenhouse and nursery plants.

Current forestry research evaluates the growth rates of conventional and paraplow planted pine trees. Loblolly pine planting determines what species of insects affect tree growth.

Major studies of agriculture and forest water quality are being conducted. Quantity and quality of all inputs which include both natural occurring and production inputs are measured. Ground water contamination and input movements are observed.

Turfgrass research is the most recent project at the Sandhills Research Station which is an appropriate site due to its soil type, close proximity to major recreational golfing areas, and a local need for increased research on turfgrass production.

Livestock research focuses on a controlled grazing program, as well as other programs involving forages both for grazing and feed sources.

Individual and group feeding facilities are used to investigate the effects that different feeds and forages have on lactating cattle and heifers. Various forage production experiments are performed for their use in both heifer and lactating animal forage grazing trials.

The poultry research program involves the use of both layers and broiler breeders. The Piedmont Research Station in Salisbury is currently the only site for the Layer Performance Management Test in North Carolina. Poultry research projects include egg holding studies, pullet growth and development trials, layer diet evaluations, layer molt nutrition trials, broiler breeder development and performance students and egg processing research projects. The composting facility is used to research the most effective ways of composting poultry mortalities in an environmentally safe manner.

The latest methods in swine production are explored such as new concepts in facilities, environmental control, materials handling systems, and especially, waste management. Recommended practices related to breeding, sow selection, herd health, and balanced feed ration programs are demonstrated, and detailed management records assist in the refinement of these practices.

Additional applied research such as disease and pathogen control, and split-sex feeding is conducted.

Many Success Stories

The dedicated efforts of our research station personnel have resulted in many remarkable success stories. Here are just a few.

At Castle Hayne, we've produced new blueberry varieties that are productive, well adapted to North Carolina growing conditions and, very important, are resistance to stem canker and stem blight diseases. Furthermore, they taste good.

Tomatoes have become an important cash crop in Western North Carolina, and at our research station there we've bred new varieties of tomatoes which are productive and resistant to disease. Work at the mountain research station has resulted in improved cattle quality and the first two burley tobacco varieties released in North Carolina were produced at the mountain research station.

Development of the first tobacco varieties resistant to Granville Wilt and black shank disease and the invention of tobacco bulk curing barns occurred at the Oxford Tobacco Research Station.

The hills of the northern Piedmont area of North Carolina are plagued with highly erodible top soils. The solution we found to this problem was no-till and minimum tillage cultivation techniques which have resulted in significantly less erosion. Production on our no-till experiment tracks have consistently out performed conventional tillage control plots by margins of 2-to-1 in corn yields for more than a decade. Studies continue to advance our knowledge about no-till techniques.

Scientists at the Sandhills Research Station are optimistic about the development of new soybean varieties that will perform better than existing varieties during drought conditions.

At the Tidewater Research Station, a herd of 100 pure-bred Black Angus brood cows are being studied to examine beef production. Preliminary work already has resulted in calf weaning weights that have increased 50 percent.

As a direct result of the work of these research stations, more crops are grown per acre today and larger, healthier animal litters are raised throughout North Carolina than ever before.

Standards

The Standards Division is a regulatory division responsible for enforcing the North Carolina Weights and Measures Act, the Gasoline and Oil Inspection Law, and the LP-Gas Inspection Law. Inspectors in the Measurement Section are responsible for testing, weighing and measuring packaged goods for compliance with their net contents statement. Examples of inspections performed by this section are scales in grocery stores, gasoline dispensers at service stations, meters on delivery trucks, truck scales at grain elevators, and packages in grocery stores.

The Motor Fuels Section inspectors are responsible for testing motor fuels and certain other petroleum products for compliance with the law and rules adopted by the Gasoline and Oil Inspection Board. This section is concerned with petroleum properties like octane, water contamination, lube oil viscosity, and flash point of kerosene. The LP-Gas Section inspection staff is responsible for inspecting LP-Gas (propane) installations and transportation vehicles for compliance with the LP-Gas Inspection Law.

In addition, the section performs safety inspections of anhydrous ammonia installations. Another important Division service is the measurement services provided by the Standards Laboratory Section to support both commercial weights and measures systems and the industries of North Carolina. This section performs precision mass, length, volume, and temperature measurement services on a fee basis.

When violations of the law or rules are discovered, the Standards Division takes a variety of actions. First-time and less severe problems are dealt with through stop-sale and stop-use orders. Repeat problems and those dealing with willful violations are usually handled through civil and criminal penalty actions as provided by law. In recent years, civil penalty assessments have played a prominent role when stores continue to have unacceptably high price scanning error rates.

In a typical year, Standards Division staff will inspect some 35,000 scales, more than 80,000 motor fuel dispensers, 1,100 price scanning systems, 7,000 fuel oil and LP-Gas meters, and 780 grain moisture meters. Also more than 21,000 octane determinations and some 4,000 engine oil viscosity determinations are made each year.

Veterinary

Animal health has been a major concern of North Carolina livestock and poultry farmers for two centuries. One outbreak of disease can destroy an entire herd. Brucellosis, pseudorabies, tuberculosis and equine infectious anemia are some of the major health programs. When infected animals are found, measures are taken to separate them from the rest of the herd and take the appropriate action to keep the disease from spreading while disease eradication occurs. This is accomplished with the legislative authority to place quarantines on premises infected or exposed to diseases. It has been the responsibility of the Commissioner of Agriculture to commission persons within the Veterinary Division to place and manage quarantines. A quarantine requires that a sign be posted at the road and a written notice be issued to the herd owner restricting the movement of the animals in such a way as not to cause undue risk of exposure of disease to animals or man.

Diseases such as tuberculosis and brucellosis are controlled and eradicated because they are infectious to both men and animals. Diseases like Pseudorabies, Equine Infectious Anemia and Hog Cholera are controlled or eradicated because they are of concern to all persons in that these diseases can spread from farm to farm, threatening the food source and animal populations of our state as well as our ability to trade meat and poultry products, biologics and live animals or embryos with other states and nations.

Inspectors from the Meat and Poultry Inspection Service are stationed at meat packing plants to ensure that meat is clean and disease-free. Public perception of the wholesomeness and safety of our food resources as always dramatically effects demand for our agricultural products. Diseased animals are rejected at slaughter plants. Unfit food is withdrawn from the market. Meat and poultry inspection is changing to strengthen consumer confidence through the technological advances of testing for bacteria and residues.

The Department's diagnostic laboratories analyze dead animals to determine the cause of death or disease. This is what is necessary for disease prevention and control. There are seven diagnostic laboratories located strategic to the animal populations within the state. These labs perform such functions as toxicology, pathology, bacteriology, histology and virology.

Hog Cholera

Hog Cholera was North Carolina's major livestock problem when I became Commissioner of Agriculture. Remembering my childhood experience of seeing the terror in my mother's face when she learned that all of our hogs--which was the meat for several families for a year -- had to be destroyed, I pledged to make the eradication of this dreadful disease my number one goal.

It was not an easy task, nor a popular one. In retrospect now that we have accomplished that goal and not a single case of hog cholera has been reported in North Carolina in 23 years, it seems entirely unlikely than anyone would oppose such a worthy endeavor. As with any effort to remove a disease from a population, there were a number of opponents of the effort.

Some of the most esteemed agricultural professors at my beloved alma mater were cool to the idea because they did not think it possible in the first place. Secondly, there is a notion among scientists that it may not be a good thing to eradicate a species even if it is harmful and serves no useful purpose in the scheme of things.

Some veterinarians were actively opposed to the proposal because they made a good living administering cholera immunizations. They were not at all supportive of a program, which if succeeded, would wipe out a major source of their income. However, these kinds of endeavors are the backbone of the sign in my office "90% Attitude and 10% Effort." Anything is too difficult for the person who can find excuses for not trying.

Background

The outbreak of hog cholera reached its peak in this country in 1969 when the U. S. Department of Agriculture reported paying more than $6.5 million in indemnities to farmers whose infected animals were destroyed.

Hog cholera is a viral disease which affects only swine. Although highly contagious to swine, it has no relationship to the disease known as Asiatic cholera of humans which is caused by bacteria.

Based on what we know about hog cholera, it is apparently a native American disease. The first incidence of the disease was noted in 1833 in southern Ohio along the Muskingum River. From here it spread throughout the United States and the rest of the world, killing more swine than any other infectious disease yet known.

The name "hog cholera" stems from confusion created by an outbreak of Asiatic cholera in humans that coincided with the first incidence of hog cholera with both the common symptoms of fever and diarrhea. Hog cholera is sometimes referred to as "swine fever."

During the last half of the 19th century, hog cholera threatened to destroy the entire swine industry of the United States. In the three decades from 1884 to 1913 hog cholera killed nearly 10 percent of the entire swine herd in America. In communities where entire herds were killed, the impact was devastating to farmers and their families who depended on swine for a major source of their food and income.

The cause of hog cholera was not discovered until 1903. Within five years, the U. S. Department of Agriculture had developed an anti-hog cholera serum that would protect hogs for the disease. The serum could be used simultaneously with the disease-causing virus to produce a long-lasting immunity.

Although the virus-serum method of immunization was quick, there were inherent dangers. Hogs treated by this method, though immune themselves, continued to shed the virulent virus for some time and thus could infect other animals. The irony was that the virus of immunizing hogs, unless handled property, provided an additional means of spreading the disease. Vaccination was not a universal practice because some growers chose not to protect their herds and instead took a chance that the disease would not strike. Many lost this gamble and hog cholera continued to spread.

In 1961 the U. S. Congress passed Public Law 87-209 which directed the Secretary of Agriculture to carry out a nationwide eradication program in cooperation with the states. In 1962 a four-phase program was established that outlined the various steps which would eventually lead to complete eradication of the hog cholera virus in the United States. North Carolina enacted its own law, at my request, to increase testing and restrict the movement of infected animals. It was estimated that the cost of the eradication program to the federal government would range from $160 million to $200 million. The actual cost was $140 million. However, losses to hog cholera during the decade of the eradication program would have exceeded $1 billion.

In North Carolina we cooperated with the federal initiative to eradicate hog cholera and added our own sense of urgency. By 1968, we reached a very significant milestone in that during the month of June no new outbreaks of hog cholera were reported. That was the first month in more than a century for such a feat.

By 1972, we had achieved our goal. Prior to March 1, 1972, only one case of hog cholera had been reported in North Carolina in nine months. Then ten cases of hog cholera were discovered apparently stemming from an out-of-state livestock dealer who sold the infected animals to buyers here.

I am proud to say that hog cholera is no longer a threat to North Carolina farmers and that is a major reason that the production of pork has become our state's leading cash income crop.

State Fair

The annual North Carolina State Fair has been a highlight of the North Carolina farm year for more than a century. While the Fair is still a major event, it is only one activity at the State Fairgrounds where a variety of events year around draw several hundred thousand citizens a year. In addition to the State Fair, they come to the fairgrounds to attend ice shows and professional hockey games at Dorton Arena. Many fine exhibitions such as home and garden shows, farm machinery shows and a variety of hobby events featuring such enthusiasts as computer experts, gun collectors and Civil War buffs are held each year. The weekly flea market on Saturdays and Sundays attracts several thousand buyers and lookers.

Altogether these events bring more than a million people a year to the North Carolina State Fairgrounds.

Attendance at the 1996 State Fair totaled 759,429, some 60,000 more than the previous year. Two new exhibits--"Cyber Space" and "Down on the Farm"--were big attractions. Cyberspace visitors could access the Internet and learn how the North Carolina Department of Agriculture uses computer technology to work more efficiently. More than 175,000 people visited the technology exhibit.

At the "Down on the Farm" exhibit, audiences saw a farmer character consuming locally grown commodities on a trip around the farm.

The North Carolina State Fair has been an important means for the farmer to display his best products and learn about the latest farm technology for more than two centuries. In 1749 the General Assembly passed an act providing for a "Colonial Fair" and selected a site in Northampton County in the town of "Hawns" and set the site of future fairs. Subsequent fairs were held in Halifax and Edenton.

Early fairs were a combination of celebrations of harvest and farm exhibitions. There were wrestling matches, horse races, and unique shows to please the crowds, along with the serious display of outstanding examples of good farming. In the time before radio and television, the State Fair became one of the most effective ways for farmers to exchange ideas and learn about new techniques for improving their productivity.

The first real State Fair was held in Raleigh in 1853, sponsored by the State Agricultural Society. The Society held the fair annually until the outbreak of the Civil War in 1861. From then until it dissolved in 1926, the fair was sponsored and conducted by the Society. It had an uncertain future for the next decade until W. Kerr Scott, pledged during his campaign for commissioner that the State Fair ought to be taken over by the state and managed by the North Carolina Department of Agriculture as an official way to promote North Carolina farm products.

In one of his first acts as Commissioner, Scott kept his pledge and hired Dr. J.S. Dorton of Shelby as the Fair's first professional manager. North Carolina's State Fair thrived under his diligent and energetic leadership. He implemented many of the great events and activities we continue today and which helped build the State Fair into one of the most important annual celebrations of agriculture in North Carolina. Dr. Dorton kept the post 36 years, until his death in 1961.

Commissioner L.Y. Ballentine assumed the role as Fair manager in 1961 and performed those duties along with his major responsibilities as Commissioner until his death in 1964. I appointed Bob Shoffner Fair Manager in 1964 and Art Pitzer in 1965. In 1967, I named Sam Rand to the post and he became my good friend and colleague for three decades until his untimely death in 1997, just a week before the opening of the 1997 State Fair.

The North Carolina State Fair is many things to many people. It is a place of fun and frolity for the many children who arrive each year from all over North Carolina. It is a place of curiosity to many who have not grown up or lived and worked on a farm. For the farmers, the North Carolina State Fair is still the best place to demonstrate to all of our people the vital importance of the work we do in agriculture.

Chapter 5

Marketing

Getting the farmer's produce from his field to the consumer's table in the form of a fair exchange is as important as growing the crops. Otherwise there is no reason to plant and harvest a surplus.

When I first became Commissioner of Agriculture, some 30 years ago, the importance of developing a successful marketing program for North Carolina farmers and their products loomed as one of the great challenges that must be met if we were to realize our fullest potential as a great farm state. Growing up on my father's farm in Rowan County I saw, at an early age, that we could have the very best crops and livestock, and yet without a good market, realize only a limited return from our work and investment.

Other Commissioners deserve credit for first recognizing and taking important first steps to lay a foundation for building the successful programs that exist today. W. Kerr Scott advanced important marketing initiatives as Commissioner of Agriculture and later, as Governor, launched North Carolina's most aggressive campaign of building farm-to-market roads in the state's history. Before the era of good roads it cost more to ship a bushel of corn from central North Carolina to the coast than its market price.

Leonidas Polk, our first Commissioner, returned from the Civil War with a vision that North Carolina farmers could create a better life for themselves and their families by selling their surplus farm products and earning money to buy other goods and services they could not grow. Commissioner Polk was ahead of his time.

During my tenure as manager of the Raleigh Farmers' Market, many of the experiences I encountered there were good lessons in marketing. At the farmers' market, I became aware of the marketing needs of the small farmer who knew how to grow squash, green beans and tomatoes, but often was at a loss as how to best market his product.

During this same period of time, I developed a close working relationship with two giants in the food industry, Colonial Stores and Winn Dixie. I remember Steve Wilson, produce buyer for Colonial telling me one day, "Jim, if you don't sell it, you smell it!" Basically, Steve was telling me that a good marketing program is absolutely essential and it is a process which requires quick decisions and a degree of risk.

I want to pay tribute to four marketing directors who played important roles in achieving diversification and leadership in the marketing arena. They are John Winfield, Curtis Tarleton, Charles Elks and Wayne Miller. Each of these four directors gave different visions for the future of North Carolina's Agriculture. Three of them served as National Presidents of the respective position. Winfield, Tarleton, and Miller all served as National Presidents of NAAMO. North Carolina farmers and consumers who benefit today from our successful marketing programs are indebted to each of these dedicated professionals who pioneered, along with me, many new and exciting marketing innovations.

It became apparent early during my tenure as Commissioner that an effective marketing program was vital to another important goal, diversification.

In development of our marketing program I have always strived to shape an agricultural marketing strategy that would provide marketing tools for the small and medium size farmer, as well as the large farmers. I also envisioned a partnership approach that would help local farmers sell their products to local folks. Why buy white potatoes from another state? I wanted to develop a good working relationship with food chains, restaurants, military installations, schools, prisons, wholesale operations---all of these and more.

North Carolina is fortunate to be centrally located on the east coast, within a few hours' drive of several large urban markets. This presents a unique opportunity for our farmers who can pick fresh produce in the early morning hours and have it in the marketplace by late afternoon.

Much of our initial marketing efforts focused on crops, particularly tobacco. However, I always have had a special commitment to seeing that we realized our fullest potential for growing and selling livestock. Even in the 60s I knew that North Carolina would someday be a major player in that arena. Our livestock growth has been phenomenal due to a lot of factors.

As I think back over these 30 years I recall, with great affection, the combined efforts of our commodity groups, N.C. Farm Bureau, N.C. State's great Research and Extension Service, the young minds of 4H and FFA and the support for all our agriculture business industry that committed to making our state the best and supported our marketing efforts throughout the 30-year span. We could not have achieved our goals without the enthusiastic and coordinated efforts of all these organizations. I also want to mention the role of our media folks-certain key leaders including Ray Wilkinson, Johnny Hood and many others who got behind all our programs.

I want to tell you, section by section, of the achievements of our marketing division. The story of our marketing efforts includes special programs in Livestock, Market News, Domestic Marketing, Horticulture Marketing and International Trade.

Domestic Marketing

Domestic marketing is a vital link to the success of producers and agribusiness. If you can't sell at home in the United States, where can you sell? Domestic markets not only take the crops and livestock of large producers, but also give us the opportunity to help small producers and companies as well. This has always been a goal of mine. Therefore, I have always placed a great deal of emphasis on expanding existing markets and developing new ones for our farmers.

From the beginning, it was apparent that we needed to work directly with producers and help them sell their product. In order to do this, the North Carolina Department of Agriculture had to have a strong relationship with retailers, food service suppliers, and wholesalers. It also meant educating producers and companies in marketing.

The first step was to develop a plan to bring all the elements together. We thought we were doing all the right things and setting the world ablaze. What we were doing was laying the foundation for the best program in the country. As a result of those early efforts and a lot of hard work, we have been recognized by several prestigious national organizations as an agricultural marketing leader in the United States. For example, the Food Marketing Institute, which is the leading food organization in the world, recently recognized us at their annual conference as the most productive marketing division in the country.

I've traveled across North Carolina many times--from mountain tops to coastal marshes--meeting with buyers and producers. Today we see the benefit of those years of foundation. We work with companies just getting started by helping with packaging, arranging buyer meetings, researching markets, and setting up shows to attract buyers. We also help the larger companies that seek to develop markets in other parts of the United States.

Currently we run promotions with retailers that move tons of North Carolina products in thousands of stores. Those promotions have had a major effect on our growers and producer's ability to move their products. I am confident those measures have resulted in buyers' decisions to buy North Carolina products instead of farm products grown in other states and other countries. Also, our aggressive marketing strategy provides the best product available to the consumers of North Carolina and the United States.

"Goodness Grows in North Carolina" is a program that just makes sense. Identify top quality home grown products to the consumer, and they will buy them. There is a lot of pride in this state. The people here want to support their neighbors, and they also know that products are fresher when they are home grown. Therefore, we developed the GGINC program as a state pride program to inform the public and to let the buyers know that here are many other good North Carolina products they need to carry. Currently, there are some 550 member companies and producers representing 5,000 products who believe in the benefits of the Goodness Grows program and the participation is growing. All North Carolinians should share a great deal of pride in this program which not only helps our state's economy but is a symbol of good quality food products.

Our marketing efforts do not stop here. In 1982, we developed the concept of taking North Carolina companies to other states, and introducing them to the buyers from those areas. This was a bold new venture at that time. This was a first, unheard of, effort to take a group of North Carolina farmers and wholesales and invade another area of the country. We coined the phrase, "Flavors of North Carolina" as an identity for the show. The first show was planned and, of all things, was to take place on a river boat in Cincinnati, Ohio. We contacted the buyers and got them to agree to attend. I'm sure a lot of them agreed out of curiosity. We invited potential buyers to come see what North Carolina had to offer. After that boat left the dock, I knew we had them. Unless they were going to swim to shore, they had to listen to what we had to offer. That water is cold and swift flowing down the Ohio River!

That show was a tremendous success. With that event, we learned that you have to make the event special, something above and beyond all the other shows that are out there. We rent the ballroom of a major hotel, offer a heavy hors d' oeuvre cocktail reception complete with entertainment, and invite the buyer's spouse along for an evening of North Carolina hospitality. Why invite the buyer's spouse, you might ask. If they like the products, the buyer will give it a shot in their stores. I've seen it happen time after time.

Currently, we have around six shows a year all over the east coast. These shows produce an average of $38 million in sales for the companies attending. Now there is a waiting list for companies to take part in the shows which are funded mostly by the participating companies.

Our small retail and food service marketing staff does a tremendous job of providing assistance to farmers and agribusiness companies. They make our promotional programs successful, and influence the decisions of the buyers in the marketplace. They do this by gaining the respect of the stores and suppliers by matching them with quality products. We don't just go out and move products regardless of the quality. If it doesn't make the grade, we work with the farmers or companies to get them up to speed. Then we help farmers gain a share in the marketplace.

It has become a part of our philosophy at the North Carolina Department of Agriculture that your reputation is only as good as your product. Buyers know that if we call them about a product, they can bank on it being a top quality item. If not, I want to hear about it. I'm proud to say we have a great relationship with all the supermarkets, food service suppliers, and restaurants. They are a vital link to the success of agriculture in the state.

I've been asked why we help food manufacturers in our state? The answer is simple. These folks buy a tremendous amount of raw agricultural commodities to make their products. It is just another vital marketing link in the production cycle. I have the opportunity to encourage them to buy North Carolina products, and I do every chance I get.

In summary, marketing is a major part of what we do in the North Carolina Department of Agriculture on behalf of both farmers and consumers. I am extremely proud of our success. Companies and producers fund many of these programs. In return, our companies and producers prosper, providing fine products, jobs, and revenue to the state.

International

When I became Commissioner of Agriculture in 1964, I quickly realized the importance of the international marketplace as it related to tobacco. Tobacco accounted for a large portion of our agricultural exports then and is still our number one export item today. During my first year in office one of my greatest accomplishments was persuading Japan Tobacco, then known as Japan Tobacco and Salt Monopoly, to locate their buying office in Raleigh. They were a major customer at the time and are now our number one customer for quality North Carolina leaf.

As the international demand for tobacco grew, we began looking at other commodities which had international potential. Some of our grains, cotton and other commodities were finding their way overseas more by happenstance than a concerted effort. In 1968, I appointed an individual to coordinate our efforts internationally. He quickly established himself as a source of contact for agricultural products in our state and laid the groundwork for what we have today.

During 1968, Europe was the destination for the majority of our exports. The overwhelming majority, probably 95 percent of our exports, were of the bulk variety. Break bulk was the order of the day and we were doing our best to persuade manufacturers and processors to give our products a look. As they gave us a try they were pleased with our items and our exports began to creep upward.

In the early 1970s, our efforts branched out into the Caribbean. I remembered from my days in the produce industry hearing people talk about the "cruise ship business" and I asked my people to look into the potential for supplying cruise ships with their food needs. The more we explored, the more the potential for processed foods to be shipped internationally became a reasonable goal.

I talked with my counterparts in Maryland, Virginia, South Carolina, and Georgia about marketing processed foods internationally. After much discussion we formed the Atlanta International Marketing Association (AIM) and the five states held the first ever regional trade show in Hamilton, Bermuda. The event was very successful and caught the eye of the Foreign Agricultural Service with the U.S. Department of Agriculture.

Following this successful event, the Foreign Agricultural Service (FAS) asked if I would lead a group of Southern Commissioners of Agriculture to Western Europe to look at possible markets and joint marketing opportunities. We did this and as a result of our efforts the concept of state regional trade groups was conceived. Every state in the nation now belongs to one of these trade groups and naturally we are members of the southern group, which is the Southern United States Trade Association (SUSTA). I was on the original Board of Directors and have held every office in the organization including two terms as President in the mid 80's.

After SUSTA was formed, we began shifting our marketing efforts to processed or prepared foods. We continued promoting our bulk commodities, but I felt if we could process these items in our state and ship them overseas we could get a higher dollar for the item as well as provide jobs for our people here in North Carolina.

Today, roughly one-half of our exports are high value processed foods and they are by far the fastest growing segment of our agricultural exports.

In 1975, I joined with the Governor, the Secretary of Commerce, and the Secretary of Transportation to open our first state office outside the United States. We pooled our resources and hired a director to promote our state's products, recruit industry and generate business for our state. In 1976, I placed in individual in the office in Dusseldorf, W. Germany, to develop markets for our agricultural products. We laid many important foundations, but with the changing economies around the world and after much thought we decided to service the European market from Raleigh and shift our focus to Asia.

Beginning in the early 1980s, the economies of Asia began booming and our exports of value added products were positioned to participate in the growing demand for high quality U.S. foods. Our association with Japan Tobacco opened many doors for us in Japan and once we established ourselves there we proceeded to enter other Pacific Rim and Asian markets. The Far East is now the major region for agricultural products from our state. I believe the greatest growth market for our food and fiber is Asia and the majority of our marketing monies are focused on the big emerging economies of Asia.

I learned early during my tenure as Commissioner that in order to sell to someone you must deal with them face to face and as a result of that I have lead trade missions to Germany, Belgium, the Netherlands, the United Kingdom, Sweden, Denmark, Japan, Taiwan, Australia, New Zealand, Mexico, Argentina, Brazil, Venezuela, and Canada. Some of my fondest memories have occurred in some of the most remote corners of the globe. I have eaten everything from moose lips to fish eyes, duck tongue to pig spleens, and raw fish to beef tripe, while all the time telling people of the fine North Carolina products we have available for export.

Once in China, in the early 1980's, I had been there for seven days and had no idea what I had eaten. Upon our arrival in Hong Kong I told one of my associates, "I am going to have a piece of good beef and I don't care if it costs me 50 dollars." Fifty dollars was a lot of money in 1981. He found us a small ordinary type steak house, we ordered, we ate and we enjoyed. The bill was $62.50 each. We looked at each other and I said, "It was worth every damn dime."

International markets hold tremendous potential for the farmers of our state. We must remember that 95 percent of the people on the earth live outside the boundaries of the United States and we must cultivate these markets if this great industry which I represent is to grow and survive. The great potential for future growth in North Carolina agriculture belongs to the companies with the vision to look overseas. I have seen bonuses made and businesses rebound as the result of the international transactions.

Much has been said about the North American Free Trade Agreement (NAFTA), the General Agreement on Tariffs and Trade (GATT), and the World Trade Organization (WTO). I am proud to say I was the first Commissioner of Agriculture in the country to publicly endorse NAFTA. Many of my colleagues asked, "Jim, have you lost your mind?" No, I haven't lost my mind.

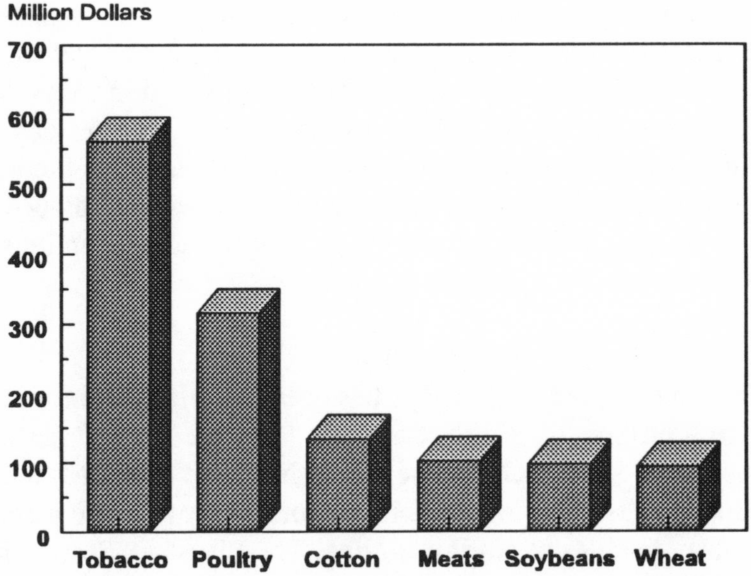

North Carolina Major Export Commodities, 1996
Table 7

I have always believed that trade builds friendships and creates peace. An old friend of mine who worked in Mexico for fifty years told me something which has really stuck with me. He said the Mexicans only had to look over the border to the north to see what the good life was like and they are determined to have a piece of the pie. He went on to explain that we could ignore them, but they would come to our country in droves unless we agreed to help them build their economy. Yes, I am proud to have been an early supporter of NAFTA and I firmly believe Mexico will be one of our major trading partners by the year 2000.

I have met or received heads of state, corporate presidents, and government officials and I have found we may have many differences but we all generally agree that the future is for the internationalist. We used to say we were within a day's drive of the major markets in the United States. Today with the proposed Global TransPark, which I believe and hope will become a great success, we are only a day away from any market in the world. We must look forward and let our imagination run wild as we explore possibilities for our products.

Twenty years ago I said there is no sector of the economy more affected by international trade than agriculture, yet many farmers and agribusinesses know less about the world markets than most. Today the vibrant industry of agriculture is on the cutting edge of opening markets all over the globe. By early in the next century, I believe a majority of our production will be shipped to other countries. That explains, in part, why I am so optimistic about the future of agriculture in this state.

Livestock

The livestock industry always has been important to me and to the farm income of North Carolina. At the time I became Commissioner of Agriculture, we had a sheep and cattle marketing program and a world of opportunity to positively affect the income of the farm families of North Carolina. The Livestock Section has excelled in the development of innovative marketing programs that assist the livestock producers. My sincere thanks to H.D. Quessenberry, retired section chief, and Chuck Miller, current Livestock Section head, for the progressive commitment of fulfilling my vision of effective local, state, national and international marketing avenues for North Carolina livestock. The development of concise grade standards for live animals and the accurate implementation of these grades, coupled with identification and selection of superior genetics for optimal animal production have been key factors in the success by our livestock marketing staff in propelling programs to a most envious position throughout the nation. The following is a species by species synopsis of the livestock programs and a few highlights of each.

The feeder cattle marketing program began 30 years ago, and continues to be one of the most important programs within the department. Most of North Carolina's feeder cattle producers sell calves only once a year and it is imperative that we do our utmost to assure that these producers obtain the best possible price for these cattle. In the late 1960s, there was very little continuity among the feeder cattle marketing programs of different states and therefore no consistency in descriptions of these cattle, which resulted in a considerable discount in price for our southeastern calves and yearlings. In a cooperative program with USDA, North Carolina was the first state to adopt a muscle thickness grading system for feeder cattle. This program was the developmental stage of the current L-M-S system which is now used throughout the USA.

Implementation of this grading system in the state graded feeder cattle sales and the on farm truck load lot sales insures that our producers will receive the premium price for the quality they produce.

In 1967, we started the first graded feeder pig sales with a total of four sales marketing about 3,000 feeder pigs. After 12 years and many innovations, in 1978, our staff individually graded and marketed more than 860,000 feeder pigs through the North Carolina State Graded Feeder Pig Sales. As with the feeder cattle program, the NCDA livestock staff assisted USDA with developing the national feeder pig grade standards and our program has been used as a model for which other states have patterned their feeder pig marketing programs. In 1969, the market hog program was initiated resulting in higher prices paid for superior carcass hogs. These swine marketing programs were the stepping stones of the most economically important animal industry in North Carolina today...hogs. I am very proud of our hog industry and especially by the fact that North Carolina is the nation's second largest producer of hogs.

The wool pools or cooperative grading and sale of the wool produced in North Carolina is small compared to the cattle and swine programs, but economically important to our sheep producers and a contributing factor to their income. Our staff continues this program along with a graded lamb marketing program.

A unique program until recent years is the meat goat program. We were the first state to begin a graded meat goat sale and to many it is surprising that the first graded goat sale was in North Carolina in 1978. Our goat marketing program was at first a means for dairy goat producers to market their surplus and buck kids, however within the last couple of years, goat marketing responsibilities have been assigned to the livestock marketing staff and we are currently working in a cooperative program with USDA and VDAC to develop uniform slaughter grade standards for meat goats. There is potential in North Carolina for meat goats to add diversity and income to the livestock industry.

In 1970, little was being done to assist the growing horse industry in our state. After meeting with several horse producers and discussing the possibilities and problems associated with horse marketing and the related economic impact to North Carolina, I assigned the first horse specialist in North Carolina to my marketing staff. Progress during the last 16 years has resulted in unprecedented growth of our horse industry.

I strongly support expanded international markets, and even with the complexities associated with live animal exports, this also is a very significant program of the livestock section. It was during 1973 that I made the decision that the Department was going to actively pursue overseas markets for breeding stock, and since that first plane load of breeding swine to the Dominican Republic, the basis of our International livestock program has been to assist North Carolina producers to market the best possible genetics of unquestionable performance and health. Diligence and determination have resulted in successful marketing of North Carolina dairy and beef cattle, horses, swine, goats and sheep throughout the world. During the drought of 1986 when our cattle producers were faced with short feed supplies and depressed local and national prices, my staff marketed about 2,500 dairy heifers to South America, Central America, and Pacific Rim countries. We continue this quest of the world markets as an additional avenue for the production of our livestock operations.

The program that has had and continues to have the greatest impact on the total livestock industry of North Carolina is the livestock events at the State Fair. During my administration unprecedented growth has occurred in the livestock shows. The livestock staff has complete responsibilities of the North Carolina State Fair at Raleigh livestock shows and sales, and the new Mountain State Fair at Fletcher livestock events. In the late 1970s and early 1980s, I gave the authority to the livestock staff to pursue and develop events especially for the youth of North Carolina. This has proven to be a monumental advancement of North Carolina's livestock industry. From 18 livestock shows and about 500 entries in the mid 1970s, we have increased to 80 livestock shows and more than 4,000 entries at the State Fair. The youth exhibitors from North Carolina are provided exclusive shows for Market Steers, Market Lambs, Market Barrows, Market Meat Goats, Beef Heifers, Dairy Heifers, and Ewe Lambs. I am a firm believer that youth livestock events build strong character and solid foundations for the next generation of North Carolina livestock producers. These youth shows and sales at the State Fair also contribute approximately one third of a million dollars per year to the youth exhibitors. In addition to the State Fair, my livestock staff is in the process of developing similar programs at the Mountain State Fair.

I love the livestock industry of North Carolina and during the past 30 years I have been insistent on a livestock marketing staff that has the attitude and ability to develop and implement a total livestock marketing program, keep abreast of ever changing genetic advancements, and provide marketing assistance to any producer in North Carolina, whether it be a family farm or a multi thousand head operation.

I am deeply appreciative to all the people, literally hundreds of dedicated career employees and volunteers, who have worked diligently over the years to help create such a fine agricultural marketing program that has meant much to both the farmers of North Carolina and to our consumer citizens.

Cotton

Cotton has always been an important crop in North Carolina, both economically and politically. The price of cotton and problems with its growth and production have fluctuated widely. At the time I became Commissioner, the crop was well below its historic peak of production. By 1960, there had been a decline in acreage for some time. In 1964 there were 395,000 acres planted in the state, quite a bit less than during the roaring twenties when well over a million acres of cotton were planted in North Carolina. A few years after that cotton almost became extinct in the state. The boll weevil had infested our cotton crop and pretty much wiped us out of business.

It was always very important to me to help our producers grow the best crop they could and receive the highest returns. I made eradication of the boll weevil a top priority of my administration and became determined to get rid of that pest. Legislation was passed in 1975 and a trial boll weevil eradication program was begun. By 1987, the eradication phase was successfully completed and the monitoring program took over from there. Since then our cotton acreage has grown to more than 800,000 acres in 1995. Dedicated members of the cotton industry and strong marketing programs have placed cotton back on the throne as "King Cotton." My goal is to see a million acres of cotton planted and harvested in North Carolina.

The "Green" Industry

The greenhouse and nursery business in North Carolina has made enormous progress during the past three decades. In 1960, there were a handful of genuine retail garden centers in the state's major cities of Charlotte, Raleigh, and Greensboro and a very few production nurseries growing field-grown, woody ornamentals balled in burlap. Some bulb growers existed in Eastern N.C., and a few glass greenhouses produced both cut and potted flowers. Farm supply stores handled a few "pull-plants" and that was about it.

As our demographics began to evolve and become more urban, it was apparent that a tremendous opportunity existed for growth in demand for all types of landscaping plants. Farmers began to experiment with small polyethylene covered greenhouses and plastic-potted ornamentals. The "Green Revolution" had begun. In the early 70s, mass merchants such as Sears, K-Mart and Lowes entered the game and plant sales exploded. We knew that our sunlight transmission was among the best in the country and how critical this was to floral production. Coupled with our Mid-Atlantic shipping location, I knew we were poised to become a major player in the greenhouse and nursery business.

In the past 30 years, the greenhouse and nursery industry in North Carolina has grown from 1.5 percent of our agricultural production to more than 13 percent. Our "green industry" has been the fastest growing segment of our agricultural economy and we are third in the nation in total production.

Today, the North Carolina Department of Agriculture provides marketing assistance and nursery inspections to more than 1500 certified nurseries. The Marketing Division assists the North Carolina Association of Nurserymen and the North Carolina Commercial Flower Growers Association in conducting trade shows and marketing promotions to increase sales of these products. Our marketing specialists serve as advisors to the Boards of Directors of both organizations. We now market North Carolina grown plants in all states east of the Mississippi and Canada. Currently we are working to develop the virtually untapped market for field grown cut flowers.

Apples

North Carolina's some 300 commercial growers produce in excess of 135 million pounds of apples for fresh and processed markets with a value of more than $20 million a year. Apples are grown primarily in western North Carolina on approximately 10,000 acres concentrated in Henderson, Haywood, Lincoln and Alexander counties.

The NC Apple Growers Association was formed in 1953 to promote and encourage the intelligent and orderly production and marketing of apples and apple products.

With funds collected through a voluntary assessment, a number of programs are developed to promote North Carolina fruit. They fund booths at the Flavors of Carolina Food Shows, the MDI Food Show, the United Fresh Fruit and Vegetable Conference and a number of fairs and festivals across the state. They also help to fund the Farm Bureau Marketing program, the "5 A Day Program" and the International Apple Institute.

Many years ago I saw the need to recognize a firm or organization that excels in promoting and distributing fruits and vegetables. That firm is honored each year at the United Fresh Fruit and Vegetable Conference with what has become known as the Commissioner's Award for their efforts in promoting and distributing fruits and vegetables. In 1996, Gary Davis, then the current President of the NC Apple Growers Association, received the Commissioner's award for the accomplishments of the Association.

North Carolina ranks seventh in apple production in the United States. Some 40 percent of the state's crop is marketed as fresh apples through packing/shipping operations and direct marketing outlets. The remaining 60 percent is used in the processing industry, mainly as applesauce and juice.

Four major varieties make up the bulk of North Carolina's apple production--Rome, Red Delicious, Golden Delicious and Stayman. However, more than 40 other varieties are grown on a limited basis. These include new cosmopolitan varieties such as Gala, Fuji, Empire, Ginger Gold, Jonagold, and Muntzu. Antique varieties such as Arkansas Black, Grimes, Limber Twig, Virginia Beauty, and Wolf River are also still available.

The fastest growing section of the apple industry is the roadside apple market which offers locally grown crisp, sweet and juicy apples, as well as additional products and services to both the local community and tourists visiting the Western North Carolina mountains in the fall. Some of these markets offer customers the opportunity to pick their own apples, watch apple cider being made and picnic as they can take a break during their afternoon drives through the scenic mountains.

Christmas Trees

Since the early 1960s, the annual wholesale value of North Carolina's Christmas trees has grown from around $5,000 to more than $90 million. The North Carolina Department of Agriculture has worked hard to meet the marketing needs of this industry. Our grading services, promotional assistance, survey information, and marketing contacts both domestically and internationally have helped build this strong industry. We have good working relationships with our Christmas tree industry.

Peanuts

Since the first peanuts were grown in North Carolina at Poplar Grove Plantation in 1795, the crop has been an important source of income for Tar Heel farmers. Over the last 30 years the peanut crop in the state has fluctuated between 170,000 and 140,000 acres.

North Carolina produces some of the finest peanuts in the world. The major type is the large kernel flavored Virginia-type peanut that is used mainly for cocktail peanuts and roasted in the shell. North Carolina produces 54 percent of Virginia-type peanuts grown in the United States. Marketing and promotion of peanuts has been greatly enhanced by the efforts of the Division of Marketing.

In 1960, peanut farmers in the state averaged 1,810 pounds per acre. In 1994, the state acreage was in excess of 3,200 pounds per acre. Much of this increase can be attributed to research done at the excellent research farms operated and maintained by the North Carolina Department of Agriculture.

In 1965, the market value of the North Carolina peanut crop was $44 million and by 1995, it was more than $140 million.

Marketing and research will be an integral part of the future for the North Carolina peanut farmer. The GATT and North America Free Trade Agreement (NAFTA) trade agreements are changing the peanut industry. With foreign peanuts having greater access to the U.S. market it will be increasingly important to promote U.S. peanuts.

Fruits and Vegetables

Fruit and vegetable production in North Carolina is the primary reason we have the third most diversified state in the country when it comes to production agriculture. While it is true that many fruit and vegetable crops have declined in total acreage over the last thirty years, there has been substantial growth in the industry overall. We now produce more sweet potatoes than any other state and rank second in production of cucumbers for pickles. Top fruit crops include fourth place rankings for strawberries and blueberries. In order to provide the most effective marketing assistance for our growers, our strategy has been modified over the years.

Marketing Specialists

When I became Commissioner of Agriculture, all the horticultural marketing specialists were working out of downtown Raleigh. Although each specialist did an excellent job of traveling around the state to visit growers and keep up with the latest issues they faced, I recognized that a more personal approach was needed. Satellite offices in the different production areas would make it possible for the marketing specialist to be more accessible and a permanent fixture in a given area. An administrative core would remain in Raleigh, while satellite offices were set up and staffed with personnel who had marketing experience with the crops in a given production area.

The first satellite office was set up in Asheville to work more closely with the apple, Christmas tree, nursery, tomato and mixed vegetable industries of western North Carolina. The office itself was housed in the Western North Carolina Farmers' Market. Later, another marketing specialist position was added to assist with these commodities and efforts to promote the market itself and recruit grower support.

The second satellite office was located is Elizabeth City in 1988, to work with the white potato, watermelon, greenhouse vegetable, leafy green and mixed vegetable industries of northeastern North Carolina. This office was complete with two marketing specialists and a secretary.

Along with the creation of satellite marketing offices, development of our state farmers' market system was taking place. As part of my strategy to reach more growers on a personal level, I expressed a need for a marketing specialist at the State Farmers' Market in Raleigh. This person would be responsible for promotions at the market as well as farm inspections and grower/seller recruitment.

The third satellite office was set up in Roseboro, to work with the mixed vegetable, blueberry and pecan industries of southeastern North Carolina. One marketing specialist and a secretary were placed in this office to work with growers in one of the most heavily farmed areas of the state.

As the trends in the marketplace changed, I strived to keep ahead of the changes that would ultimately affect our growers. The world is truly becoming a smaller place. Working with the leaders of this state, I explained that agriculture should be a part of the future and not a thing of the past. With this in mind, the North Carolina Department of Agriculture became involved with a tremendous project described as the Global TransPark. As a result of agriculture's involvement in this project, a satellite office was set up in Kinston.

The Kinston office was unlike any other satellite office in that the marketing specialist here was to assist in developing agricultural products that would benefit from air freight available at the Global TransPark. In addition to this responsibility, the specialist was to develop a stronger vegetable industry.

The marketing specialists that work in these satellite offices work with each other to plan and carry out commodity promotions throughout the state and nation. These promotions serve several purposes. First and foremost, they raise awareness about a particular commodity and stimulate media attention and market demand for the item. Another benefit to working such promotions is that our marketing specialists are working side by side with the growers to promote the commodity. This is another example of the personal contact that I feel is so important. I personally enjoy many of these promotions, because they give me a chance to visit with the growers and discuss the issues they are faced with and ask how the North Carolina Department of Agriculture can help.

The value of the vegetable industry has doubled in terms of percentage of our state's total agricultural production. This increase, I believe, is a direct result of our efforts to become more closely involved with the industry on a more personal level. North Carolina produces a large portion of the safest food supply in the world, and I am proud that the Division of Marketing will be there to assist the grower with his or her marketing and distribution efforts.

Tobacco

I have often referred to tobacco as the bed rock of North Carolina's Agricultural economy. When I became Commissioner of Agriculture in 1964, tobacco grossed our producers $549 million and made up 47 percent of our total agricultural economy of $1.1 billion. In 1994, it brought in more than $942 million, and accounted for 14.8 percent of the $6.3 billion in farm income. To a large degree it has been tobacco income that enabled our producers to expand into other crops, livestock, and poultry enterprises.

The supply management program on burley and flue-cured tobacco has been highly successful. It has enabled producers to be assured of a good market and has supplied our processors, exporters, and manufacturers an adequate supply of high quality tobacco. The program has been beneficial to the entire tobacco industry.

The tobacco program has changed drastically over the past thirty years to adapt to new conditions. The switch to acreage poundage, loose leaf sales, warehouse designation, sale of quotas, and the no net cost feature are examples of how a program initiated in the 30's had been able to be an effective marketing tool in the ensuing years. It continues to be approved by growers by margins in excess of 90 percent.

In recent years tobacco has come under attack by many groups. I continue to give full support to this important commodity. It has made major contributions to many of our finest institutions and has sent literally millions of young people to our colleges and universities. I salute this industry that has been such an integral part of North Carolina's economy.

Seafood

The North Carolina Department of Agriculture is now engaged in a wide range of activities designed to greatly increase the visibility and marketability of North Carolina's seafood and aquaculture products in the domestic and international market place.

Our marketing program seeks to create a positive image in consumers' minds about the safety and health benefits of buying North Carolina seafood. To keep the public assured the seafood they are being offered is safe "Freshness from North Carolina Waters" is the seal of quality; the voice of authority the public can trust and respect to keep them informed about good seafood values and quality.

Grain

The grain industry, from both the producer and grain buyer perspective, has transformed from an era when custom grinding feed mills and grain buyers scattered the countryside to an age of consolidation and the birth of vertical integration in the swine and poultry industries. The exponential growth in the usage of grain has revolutionized the industry and led to higher revenue for producers.

Current farm legislation is leading to many changes in the agricultural sector and will force individual producers to manage their own price risk. Rather than accepting prices, producers are now managing their price risk through well established marketing practices. In 1996, the Division of Marketing launched a program to train farmers in how to manage price risk through futures and options.

With the world demand for grain products expanding, the incomes of our global trading partners increasing, and an expanding industry infrastructure lead by the end user, the individual producer is poised to reap these benefits.

Farmers' Markets

In 1954, Raleigh developer J.W. "Willie" York built the Raleigh Farmers Market which opened officially September 22, 1955, with Bob Martin serving as president and general manager. Until this time farmers sold their produce in an almost helter skelter manner. There were several small fruits and vegetable dealers scattered all around Raleigh, and a crowded downtown City Market in a deplorable condition. And thus, the Raleigh Farmers Market became the first effort to provide a central location for bringing farmers and buyers together in one area. The Raleigh market was near U.S. Highway 1 in Raleigh, located in a low, flood prone area on 18.5 acres.

In April of 1956, I was hired to be the Manager of the Raleigh Farmers Market. It was during this time that I realized more than ever that farmers needed a place to sell their produce, fruits and vegetables, and they needed to know what to expect in the way of market demands and prices. I convinced Radio Station WPTF to have an early morning and noon broadcast to give up-to-the-minute commodity pricing information to farmers every day. This kind of information is very important for a grower to know as he is harvesting his crops. Charles Edwards has continued to provide commodity prices daily on WPTF-AM Radio.

In 1958, the Raleigh Farmers Market was leased for $1 per year to the North Carolina Department of Agriculture, and I was hired to continue the operation as an employee of the state of North Carolina. After leasing for three years, the State purchased the entire property from Mr. Willie York in 1961, when it appeared he was going to sell the entire facility to dealers only at the end of the lease period. The Commissioner of Agriculture at that time, Mr. L.Y. "Stag" Ballentine, wanted to keep the market as a place for growers as well as wholesale dealers. The market continued to grow in its Central Piedmont location as it served more farmers, and eventually it became a wholesale produce terminal, local retail farmers market, garden and nursery center, farmers market restaurant, and cash and carry grocery.

The Raleigh Farmers Market became the State Farmers Market in 1961, and I continued on as market manager. One of the greatest honors for me while serving as manager of the State Farmers' Market was to be elected in 1962 as President of the National Association of Produce Market Managers, and I was honored with the title of "Market Manager of the Year" by this organization in 1964. Growth and importance to farmers within a 150-mile radius of Raleigh continued after I was appointed Commissioner of Agriculture in July 1964. Charles Murray became manager in July 1964. He continued in this position until his retirement in December 1984. Our present manager, Charles Edwards was named manager in January 1985. Mr. Edwards started working part-time as gatekeeper at the State Farmers Market in 1963, while he was a student attending North Carolina State University. Charles has been a strong leader and a good friend since he came with the Department. His leadership and efforts have made the State Farmers Market one of the best and strongest in the Southeast.

In 1991, a modern new State Farmers Market was completed and opened on Lake Wheeler Road, in Raleigh. This facility already has stretched its limits and more wholesale and retail space is in demand. Currently we have ten wholesale tenants who deliver fresh produce throughout the Piedmont daily. A large tomato packer located on the market which is open year around, seven days a week. Two restaurants serve fresh North Carolina products daily; one serves home style cooked meals, and the other serves North Carolina seafood. People stand in line daily to buy meals at each of these fine restaurants, and I highly recommend both of them.

Farmers at our markets are selling more and more plants. Today, you can find everything for your home from hanging baskets of flowers to bedding plants, greenhouse and nursery stock.

As time has moved along, population has increased in North Carolina. There are now fewer farmers than ever, yet the farmers plant more acres, and produce more per acre than ever. People have less time to grow their own gardens and fresh produce. This increased need for locally grown produce and the need for farmers to find buyers has stretched across the state.

In 1973, a feasibility study conducted in cooperation with the Western North Carolina Development Association recommended that a Farmers' Market be built in Asheville. Morris "Mac" McGough headed the Western North Carolina Development Association at that time, and he grabbed the ball and asked me to run interference in Raleigh to seek funding for the purchase of land for a Western North Carolina Farmers' Market. In 1974, area legislators supported a bill to fund the purchase of 20 acres of land from the Biltmore Estate to begin construction of a farmers' market, our second state-owned market. Clayton Davis was hired to manage and promote the development of this new facility in November of 1975. A few days before opening this new market, I asked Clayton if he thought we would ever see the truckers' shed full. He replied, "Yes, we can fill it." Surely enough it was full that very first day, and there has been an overflow to this day.

The Western North Carolina Farmers Market officially opened September 1, 1977, with one retail building and a truckers' shed. This market has continued to grow, add more buildings, and serve more than 1,200 local farmers each year with a place to sell their produce, fruit, Christmas trees, nursery plants, and herbs. This market has a flourishing garden center, restaurant, wholesale tenants, retailers, and farmers only sales area. It continues to expand in customers and growers wishing to benefit from what the market offers. It now has 37 acres, and will eventually need more space. This market has become one of the top 10 tourist stops in Western North Carolina, and one of four chosen to be featured in a nationally distributed video produced on farmers markets by the U.S. Department of Agriculture.

Certainly, it is no secret that I am especially fond of Farmers Markets, not only because of my years as Manager of the Raleigh Farmers Market, but also because I know that North Carolina farmers are proud to have these facilities where they can bring the fruits of their labor to a central location and find a waiting market with customers willing to buy. Our farmers' markets provide clean, well-maintained areas where they can display produce in an attractive and friendly atmosphere.

Mac McGough and Clayton Davis have both had a tremendous impact on agriculture in Western North Carolina, and many growers will be forever grateful for their contributions. Clayton retired in 1991 as market manager, and we named one of our local marketing specialists, Mike Ferguson, as our second market manager in January 1991. Mike is doing a great job and continues in this position today.

It is interesting to note that our farmers' markets are often used as gathering points for more than just agriculture. For instance, the Western North Carolina Farmers' Market has been used for several political rallies including Presidential candidate Walter Mondale, Gubernatorial candidate Jim Hunt, and Senatorial candidate Robert Morgan.

In the late 1970s, there was a request to establish a Farmers' Market in Charlotte. I had several meetings with the local farmers and citizens interested in this new facility, and we determined there was a real need to have a regional market in this metropolitan area. The Honorable Jo Graham Foster of the North Carolina House of Representatives went to bat for this project, and in 1981 we received funding for further study and plans. The project gained momentum, and in 1982, Charlotte Mayor Eddie Knox aided in having the City of Charlotte donate 22 acres of prime land to the State of North Carolina for the construction of a Farmers' Market. Following Mayor Knox, was Mayor Harvey Gantt, and we are thankful for his continued support for the development of this market that held a grand opening in May, 1984. We opened on gravel, and with no buildings. Frank Suddreth, a Charlotte native, was hired to spearhead the opening and promotion for the Charlotte Regional Farmers' Market, and he remains as manager today. Since 1984, we have completed several buildings and this is now a thriving business serving the local farmers and customers from the Queen City. More than 100 farmers from throughout the region come every year to find a market for their produce. A prominent wholesaler calls the Charlotte Regional Farmers' Market his home base. Several retailers based there promote fresh, local fruit and vegetables. This became our third state-owned farmers' market.

In the mid-1980s, Mr. Lindsay Cox, Executive Director of the Piedmont Triad Council of Governments, and Mr. R.N. "Buster" Linville, Chairman of the Triad Regional Farmers Market Advisory Committee were instrumental in having an economic study conducted to learn the interest and need for a Farmers Market in the Triad. Ross Williams who is now an Assistant Director of our Marketing Division, conducted the feasibility study for this region which determined that more than one million people in the Triad had very limited access to adequate quantities of locally grown fruits and vegetables. This study showed a significant demand for the farmers market in the Triad.

In 1986, we received funding from the General Assembly to purchase a site on Sandy Ridge Road determined to be centrally placed to serve the most people, and easily accessible for farmers and truckers hauling produce to and from the market. A Master Plan for a Triad Farmers Market was developed and we purchased 77 acres. "Buster" Linville made many trips to Raleigh to seek further funding, and needless to say, he kept my telephone busy. I can truly say, "Buster" is a pusher when it comes to getting something done that he believes in.

The General Assembly gave us additional funding in 1989, but before any building could be started, our funds were taken back due to a budget crunch in state funds. It was not until 1993 that we received the funds to continue with construction of this new market and in 1994 we actually broke ground. Soon after that, we hired Dexter Hill as our newest Farmers' Market Manager to come to the Triad and promote the Piedmont Triad Farmers Market throughout the region. Dexter was already with N.C.D.A. as Superintendent of our Sandhills Research Station at Jackson Springs. I told Buster, "Stop calling me at home all hours of the night, the Triad Market is being built."

Finally, after several years, our fourth farmers market is open, and more than 450 local growers have been successful in bringing their produce to the market to a crowd of hungry consumers ready to take home these delicious and fresh commodities. "Buster" was a key speaker at our grand opening ceremony, May 19, 1995, and he and his wife are regular visitors to the market since it opened. This is a very modern and attractive facility with room to grow in years to come. I feel that our immediate needs are for additional buildings that will accommodate the location of some wholesalers on the premises, thus bringing in more buyers with needs for larger quantities.

The Piedmont Triad Farmers Market is open year around, seven days a week with a family-style restaurant and a complete garden center on the site. Dexter Hill has made a fine market manager here, and we are proud of his dedication to make this market grow.

I am proud to note that all of our Farmers Markets are located on major highways, and three of them, (Western North Carolina Farmers Market at Asheville, Piedmont Triad Farmers' Market in between Winston-Salem and Greensboro, and the State Farmers' Market in Raleigh) are near exits on Interstate 40.

If I seem a bit overly enthusiastic about our farmers' markets that is because I am extremely proud of these great marketing centers for our local farmers. Few comments about our program are as rewarding as the positive comments I hear constantly from farmers who speak of the personal benefits they have enjoyed from having marketing facilities available in a location that is central to their region of the state. A recent study, conducted at the request of our Director of Marketing, Wayne Miller, revealed many facts that I have felt for years, but were not proven until now. This study was conducted by The Office of State Budget and Management's (OSBM) Management and Productivity Section. It was found that our four farmers' markets are responsible for wholesale and retail sales annually that exceed $130 million. In addition to this, there are 50 state employees, and at least 678 private sector jobs that generate income through the existence of the markets. This report states that estimates place general fund revenues as a result of farmers' markets operations at more than $6.6 million annually. These are good investments for the people of the State of North Carolina, and they have proven to be good for agriculture.

WNC Agricultural Center and North Carolina Mountain State Fair

Another important component of our Division of Marketing is the Western North Carolina Agricultural Center in Fletcher, just a few miles from Asheville. A major priority for agricultural leaders in Western North Carolina in the early 1960s, was to build a central location for livestock shows. For years, the FFA and 4-H shows had been traveling around the southwestern end of North Carolina, with no permanent home, and very often substandard facilities. Here, again, my good friend, Morris "Mac" McGough of the WNC Development Association came into the picture and convinced the General Assembly to fund the building of a permanent livestock facility if we could acquire the land.

The City of Asheville, after some prodding from "Mac," donated 25 acres of land near the Asheville Airport on which to construct the very first building for the new livestock show and sales arena, and this became reality in 1967. Soon afterwards, we constructed a youth center for overnight accommodations for exhibitors on the site.

Many beef cattle, dairy cattle, sheep and swine shows were held in this facility during the next decade, and during this time it became apparent that we needed an even larger facility to serve the agricultural community in the western region. We discussed plans, explored needs, and concluded that a combination horse/livestock arena with stalls was needed to meet the future growing requirements in this area. In 1983, a livestock/horse complex was completed with a 65,000 square foot indoor arena and 150 permanent stalls. The horse industry in North Carolina has grown by leaps and bounds, as we have an ever growing urban population seeking recreation. This segment of agriculture has benefitted North Carolina in many ways, and I see a continuing growth pattern into the future. The Honorable Liston Ramsey, of Marshall, along with other members of the General Assembly, has been very supportive of the Western North Carolina Agricultural Center, and they have made it possible to add several very important components to this complex.

Under the leadership and direction of our manager, William A. "Bill" Edmondson, the Western North Carolina Agricultural Center has continued to grow with more buildings, more stalls, more land, and more events to keep this facility busy 52 weeks of the year. It has truly become a focal point in the western region for many types of events including national, regional, state and local horse shows, cattle shows, rodeos, truck and tractor pulling contests, concerts, car sales, motor cross, mobile home shows, and even monster truck shows.

In 1985, Bill and I talked about the future for the Western North Carolina Agricultural Center, and one of the things I realized was a need in Western North Carolina for a State Agricultural Fair to provide the same caliber of agricultural fair enjoyed by thousands of people each year in Raleigh. The people of Western North Carolina very seldom travel to Raleigh for the State Fair due to distance and time required to come from such far away places as Brevard, Hendersonville, Waynesville, Marshall, Murphy, and Cherokee. It was then we sought and received funding to acquire an additional 50 acres of land adjoining the present site. We acquired this from the City of Asheville.

After several years of planning and dreaming, the North Carolina Mountain State Fair became a reality September 7-11, 1994. We started small and compact with the enclosed arena serving as an exhibit hall for both competitive and commercial exhibits. There was a cattle show, a livestock show, antique farm equipment, a heritage village, and we recognized the forestry industry with the theme "Year of the Forest." Attendance that first year was more than 45,000 and in 1995 we had a 25 percent increase.

In 1996, the third annual North Carolina Mountain State Fair was held on a completely new site under construction for 18 months. There are great expectations for continued growth here and with even more participation in livestock shows, clogging competitions, and other entertainment with the flavor of Smoky Mountain heritage. I am extremely pleased with accolades from natives of the mountains and their expressions of gratitude for this fair coming to their home area. We will keep it very much an agricultural oriented event as long as I am Commissioner of Agriculture, and we will continue to provide both educational opportunities and entertainment that will generate pride for people from all over our state, especially from Western North Carolina.

Projects Currently Being Funded and Planned

Two more projects are being planned and will soon be under construction. In Martin County, near Willamston, the Eastern North Carolina Agricultural Center will be completed early in 1998. This center will have an indoor horse arena seating 2,000, with approximately 400 stalls for horses, a multi-purpose meeting center building, and recreational vehicle sites for overnight accommodations. We have planned the design of this facility so that it will serve Eastern North Carolina in many ways for years to come. The arena will serve as a horse show facility, and also will host concerts, rodeos, equipment and auto shows, conventions, and many other events. Many of the same types of shows and events held in Fletcher will be successful also in Eastern North Carolina. This northeastern region in North Carolina has no large cities to provide the kind of facilities needed to bring in the events that this center can make possible. The economic impact of this type of agricultural center is ongoing and will continue to increase for years.

The second project is presently in the planning stage, and has already been partially funded, and we expect before the first phase is completed there will be funds from our General Assembly to complete all the components of this complex. This will be known as the Southeastern North Carolina Agricultural Center in Robeson County, and in the City of Lumberton. A beautiful site was chosen on Highway 74, just east of Interstate Highway 95. This facility will include all the necessary components of a horse arena with stalls, a multi-purpose meeting building, and a farmers market to serve the many vegetable growers that already reside in the Southeastern region of our state. There is a growing horse industry in the area, and a great need to provide a place for all the same types of events that have made the agricultural center at Fletcher so successful, plus the farmers' market and multi-purpose building. I am looking forward to having the grand opening here by mid-1998. We expect this location to provide a wholesale market on a more local basis to the many produce growers that are already established throughout Southeastern North Carolina. This will become the Agricultural Center for the region.

Market News

The Market News office is the eyes and ears of the agribusiness community in North Carolina. The staff has grown from four people in the Raleigh office to twelve across the state. Market news reporters gather price and trend data from reputable members of the business sector and analyze the results before releasing accurate unbiased price data.

In the early 1960s, reporting poultry data changed from reporting a producer price to a dock price by contacting processors. This cut back on the number of calls being made and more importantly, the industry contacts knew more about the actual market as far as supply, demand and price. The poultry industry has become integrated over the years allowing companies to produce higher quality products for the consumer by spreading cost over a large number of birds. The last few years have also brought about a change in the marketing of poultry as end users demanded the opportunity to buy selected parts instead of whole birds. Reporting of turkey data is handled on a regional basis where several states input data to make a report showing price and trend information.

Feeder pig sales began in 1965 and our experience in North Carolina became a role model for other states because every feeder pig was graded individually and not sold as a group with different grades co-mingled together. The producer got paid for what he actually produced. In past years, market hog prices were reported as a base price for live hogs at some daily buying locations. Today, hogs are sold on a carcass basis where the producer is paid for exactly the quality of hog he produces. This has allowed the producer of high yielding hogs to get a premium for his product. The size of swine farms has increased over the years and become more integrated allowing producers who are good managers to have herds of several thousand head. Hogs are now sold by the truckload and not one or two at a time. At present, two packing plants are processing about 20,000 market hogs per day. North Carolina swine are now shipped all over the world because of the excellent quality of pork produced. North Carolina ranks second in the total number of swine on farms.

Market news reporters grade and disseminate prices for about 85 percent of the livestock sold at weekly auction markets. Price and trend data is also reported at special state-sponsored cattle, goat, and sheep sales. This allows producers, processors, lending institutions, educational facilities and end users or the general public to stay informed of supply, demand and unbiased price data. The influx of non-British type cattle made for a change in grading standards during the 1970s because all cattle did not weigh the same at market time. Standards detailing frame size and muscle type were put into use to better describe the type of feeder cattle in North Carolina. The same grading standards used in North Carolina are used across the United States. This enables people from other areas to read our reports and know exactly the type, condition, and value of our livestock.

North Carolina continues to be the number one producer of sweet potatoes with some 33 percent of the U.S. market. Time has seen a great deal of change over the years. The once seasonal crop is now available all year long due to refrigeration. Blueberries, cabbage, peaches, apples and other vegetables and fruits have become big time business on a seasonal basis as more demand for quality food has come about. Daily reports on price, trend, supply and other meaningful information are released showing a FOB price.

Price data for cotton, tobacco, fish, and hay are provided with assistance from other market news offices.

The market price and trend data for all agricultural commodities are released from the Raleigh market news office. This allows for better utilization of the work force. Price information for all farm commodities is disseminated using radio, newspapers, toll-free telephones, electronic bulletin boards and the Internet. Through the use of computers the latest information can be disseminated within seconds after reports are created. At present there are about 8,000 newsletters mailed weekly, about 8,000 calls on the toll free Dial-A-Market telephone system are received each month, approximately 50 radio broadcasts are generated daily and the list of people using computer-generated reports is increasing daily. The goal of market news is for the public to ask for price data for agricultural products and we provide the official unbiased answer quickly and accurately.

Cooperative Grading Service

Grading, as a measure of quality, began in the early 1920s as the Cooperative Inspection Service under the auspices of the United States Department of Agriculture through an "agreement" with the North Carolina Department of Agriculture. These agreements later, becoming known as "Cooperative Agreements," generally covered a single commodity such as poultry or peanuts. Today the Grading Service operates on a receipt supported basis under authority contained in the Agricultural Marketing Art of 1946.

Grading and Regulatory, under the direction of Nicholas L. Paul since 1989, is also known as "The Cooperative Grading Service." These services consist of five sections: fruit, vegetable and peanut grading; poultry grading; grain grading; red meat grading and certification; and regulatory. All with the single exception of the later, operate under Cooperative Agreements between USDA (United States Department of Agriculture) and NCDA (North Carolina Department of Agriculture). The services provided to clients are on a request basis and therefore are voluntary. Clients are charged fees based on approved rates and all personnel are required to hold valid USDA licenses. Personnel assign a nationally and internationally recognized grade to agricultural products that is used as a basis for trade worldwide and the certificate is accepted as prima facie evidence of quality in all courts of law. These self-supporting programs are operated as "Trust Fund" accounts with the single exception of Regulatory. The Trust Funds were created under authority of the 1993 North Carolina General Assembly which allows for these funds to be used exclusively to operate these self-supporting programs.

The Cooperative Poultry Grading Service

The Poultry Grading Service emerged in North Carolina in the mid 1950s as a result of the authority contained in the Agricultural Marketing Act of 1946. The voluntary USDA poultry and rabbit grading program operates under these regulations and provides interested parties a national grading service based on official U.S. classes, standards, and grades. The costs involved in furnishing these grading programs are paid by the user of the service.

A mandatory egg product inspection program was also the responsibility of the Poultry Grading Service until 1996 when it was transferred to the Food Safety Inspection Service. The program requires that all egg product facilities have a full-time resident inspection service. Although North Carolina was at one time moderately involved with egg products, the industry has since relocated closer to destination markets.

The program began and remains as a tool for the industries to utilize if they choose to market their products as officially graded. Buyers and sellers can negotiate price based on U.S. Grade, official test weighing results or condition at origin and/or destination without ever seeing the products themselves. Grading provides the unbiased party to make such determinations and helps promote the sale of quality poultry products, not only in North Carolina, but throughout the world.

During the mid-1950s, the programs were offered on a limited basis, mainly fee-gradings with little or no resident graders requested in plants on a full-time basis. In 1958, Fred Pepoon was appointed to Federal-State Supervisor in North Carolina, and the Cooperative Poultry Grading Program was born.

The next 27 years were a gigantic boom for the poultry industry and the Cooperative Grading Program in North Carolina. While Fred Pepoon spearheaded the program for USDA, the state administered the grading program with expert program leadership from Guy Cutler, Larry Deal, Stone Kennett, and Laurie Wood. During this period, the program grew from the first turkey plants to install resident grading (Central Soya, Monroe and Armor, Marshville); chicken (Priebe and Sons, Concord); and shell eggs (Central Carolina Farmers, Durham) to as many as 22 plants with resident service today.

In 1985, Fred Pepoon retired and was succeeded by Stone Kennett who had previously administered the program for the State of North Carolina. Larry Deal administered the grading program for our state until 1988 at which time he retired and Laurie Wood became the program administrator.

During the 1980s, to present, the program began to grow significantly with more interest from industry in further processed items (also called value-added products) and the commodity buying program offered by USDA. During this period, grading has undergone dramatic changes in that whole carcass grading has decreased, while items such as boneless/skinless chicken breasts, thighs, and drumsticks, turkey ham, ground turkey, turkey bologna, chicken nuggets, and patties have enjoyed very good acceptance from consumers. A more diet-conscious society is turning to table fares with lower fat content as substitutes for traditional meals.

Official shell egg plants (shell egg plants that have requested a resident grader) have decreased in numbers over the past 10 years although through better technology, fewer plants can grade vast amounts of eggs. Twenty to twenty-five years ago, a machine capable of grading ninety 30-dozen cases of eggs per hour was a top-of-the-line machine that took seven to 10 people to operate.

Today, machines capable of grading 400 cases of eggs per hour are commonplace and require fewer people to operate.

In 1993, Laurie Wood left the program and Sterling Moore became program administrator. The grading program has continued to grow with the advent of new items (boneless/skinless, ham, etc.) but is experiencing some slumps associated with the economy. Cost management and providing new unexplored services to the industry are the future tools to be utilized in enhancing the grading service and the poultry industry in North Carolina.

The Grain Grading Program

The grain grading program began in North Carolina in the early 50s. John Winfield was serving as the Director of Marketing and Ollie Faison was serving as Chief Inspector.

Grain inspection in North Carolina has always operated on a permissive basis. The only mandatory inspection for grain in the United States has been for export grain.

The program began and stills remains a tool for the grain industry to buy and sell grain on the basis of official grades. Official grain grading provides a service where an unbiased person makes a determination of the quality of the grain and helps promote the sale of grain in North Carolina and the world.

In the mid-60s, Pete Lane was appointed chief inspector. Licensed grain graders at this time were Neil Morrison, Bruce Shands, Bill Parham, Edward Wester, and Staley Long. The program operated on appropriated funds at this time. In 1970, Staley Long became chief inspector and the program became receipt supported. At this time, there were 13 licensed inspectors serving the grain trade in North Carolina. Offices were located in Raleigh, Fayetteville, Greenville, Bonlee and Mocksville.

Norman McIver succeeded Staley Long in 1983. The program is presently operating with six full-time licensed inspectors in North Carolina. The bulk of the work at the present is grading soybeans going to Cargill oil refineries in Raleigh and Fayetteville. Additional work is picked up during the harvest seasons of small grain and corn.

The grain grading program remains a viable tool to the grain industry in North Carolina with the price of grain continuing to rise and the demand for quality grain in the state increasing. The service will continue to fill an important role for the grain dealers, farmers, and consumers of grain and grain products in North Carolina.

Red Meat Grading Program

In 1951, the North Carolina Legislature passed a bill setting up the meat grading and acceptance program using federal meat grading standards for the quality of beef, lamb, and veal. The purpose of the program was to work with state institutions and school systems in procurement of red meat and to provide carcass beef grading at North Carolina slaughter plants.

The acceptance program was first started to provide a service to North Carolina institutions. This program was manned by four employees who covered the state. A great part of the work involved helping county and city school systems purchase meat products. The Division of Purchase and Contract of the Department of Administration drew up a meat specification manual based on federal specifications. Approximately twenty years later, these specifications were changed to the Complete Federal Specifications, I.M.P.S., Institutional Meat Purchasing Service. These specifications are in more detail and have many more items than the old specifications manual and allowed the institutions to use competitive bidding in buying their red meat needs, thus ensuring the institution of getting the best price available.

The highlight of this program came in 1970. The State of North Carolina entered into an agreement with the U.S. Department of Agriculture to grade carcass beef in North Carolina using USDA standards and equipment. North Carolina was the first state ever to have state employees licensed by USDA to do federal carcass beef grading within the state.

This program was active until 1986 when a consolidation of beef slaughtering plants in the western United States forced slaughtering plants in North Carolina to either close or cease slaughtering and grading. The USDA school lunch program which donates ground beef to schools also contributed to a reduction in the workload. Therefore, due to circumstances beyond its control, the workforce has been reduced. In North Carolina, graders continue to work with USDA grading services to certify products.

The current purpose of this program is to work with state institutions and the Department of Correction in the procurement of red meat products purchased by the low bid system. The red meat section currently has one full-time and one part-time employee.

Beginning in 1951, the program was headed by Thomas E. Green. After the death of Green, Grover H. Dean took over as administrator until his retirement in 1982. L.T. Woodlief then became the administrator and held this position until 1992 when he was succeeded by Ed Hill.

Regulatory Programs

In 1955, Article 25 of Chapter 106 of the General Statutes of North Carolina, entitled North Carolina Egg Law, was enacted. At that time, three inspectors worked the entire state under the direction of Carl Tower. After the retirement of Tower in 1969, Guy Cutler headed the program until his resignation in 1971. Larry Tetterton was then named program administrator and served in this position until he was promoted to Assistant Director for Marketing in 1985. After Tetterton's promotion, Edgar Ingram, former Agricultural Commodity Inspector, was promoted to program administrator. Ingram headed the program until his retirement in 1994. After Ingram's retirement, Bobby Harwood was promoted to program administrator. Today the program is administered by eight full time individuals serving statewide on a regional basis.

Under the North Carolina Egg Law, regulatory personnel inspect eggs at the retail level for grade, weight, class, and temperature requirements. At non-USDA grading facilities, eggs are inspected for federal compliance. Last year, personnel visited approximately 5,537 facilities and inspected 71,760 dozen. Eggs not found in compliance are placed under stop sale provisions until reworked at the wholesale or retail level. In addition, egg displays and holding coolers are to be maintained in a sanitary manner, and a temperature of 45 degrees or less is to be maintained until purchased by consumers. Apples and peaches are also inspected for grade, weight, and labeling requirements.

In 1978, the apple and peach laws were merged with Regulatory and a surveillance position was added, providing 13 inspectors to work the state. Down sizing in government, due to the Graham-Rudman Act, began some three years later, reducing the staff to 10 individuals. Hiring freezes forced the remaining cuts down to eight. The program also has the responsibility for the apple maturity regulations, the U.S. Egg Surveillance Act, and the North Carolina egg tax laws. The latter was passed by the 1990 General Assembly and became effective October 1, 1990. This law provides for an excise tax on all eggs sold for use in North Carolina. These funds are collected and turned over to the North Carolina Egg Association for promotion.

A 300-case per hour grading machine is common today. The temperature law, 45 degrees Fahrenheit, enacted about five years ago works to the advantage of all. Today our staff devotes a great deal of time toward service, not only to producers and packers with machine or grading problems, but to consumers with regard to egg quality and safety. Also, on a weekly basis, we mail to respective packers a printout of the store inspection report. This has proven to be a valuable tool for industry.

Cooperative Grading Service

The Cooperative Inspection Service began after a "Memo of Agreement to Provide for Food Products Inspection Service" was signed April 22, 1924, and made retroactive to July 1, 1923. The agreement was signed by George R. Ross, chief of North Carolina Division of Markets. The agreement was made with the USDA Bureau of Agriculture Economics. Peanut grading began on a very limited basis around 1929.

From the 50s to the early 80s many graders followed seasons from state to state, usually from Alabama, Florida, Georgia, South Carolina, North Carolina, Virginia and Delaware. Inspectors at that time had very few benefits but could join an inspector's association that featured a newsletter and credit union established in Albany, Georgia.

Peanut inspections started about 1949 with mostly male peanut graders at that time but the trend has changed to about 95 percent female graders today.

In the 1950s, the market seasons usually started in May with strawberries in the Chadbourn, Wallace, and White Lake areas. Auction markets for vegetables were located in Clinton, Mt. Olive, Wallace, and Faison. The Faison market still operates today.

Potatoes continue to be a major vegetable crop. In 1995, 162 loads from North Carolina moved into Canadian fresh markets and a greater number into Canadian domestic markets. An additional 1,144 loads were shipped bulk for chipping, processing, or repacking into Canada. Years ago, the Aurora area was said to be the largest producer of potatoes which were often shipped on railcars. Elizabeth City also produced great volumes of potatoes in early years. The Elizabeth City and Creswell areas now produce the largest volumes of potatoes.

Christmas tree crops have increased over the last few years. North Carolina has lead the way for a Christmas tree grading system that allows for tagging trees and grading them on the stump before harvest.

The Cooperative Inspection Service has remained self-supporting since its inception from fees collected from users. The Cooperative Inspection Service, renamed Cooperative Grading Service about ten years ago, was headquartered in a rented building less than a mile from its current address. Planning began in the mid-70s for a new office building. One acre of land was purchased on May 7, 1974, for $15,000. The staff moved in the 7,200 square foot facility which cost $275,000 during August, 1976.

State supervisors, now titled program administrators, from about 1950 to present were: Gilbert Clark, W.S. Brannon, S.G. Rand, Gene Boney, Burnace Ausbon, Russell Roberson, Kenneth Perry, and currently Wayne Bryant. State supervisors were located in Raleigh until about 1979 when the office was moved to Williamston.

Resident federal supervisors include Bailey Rich, Lynn Davenport and Robert Martin. Martin has served since 1983.

The Cooperative Grading Service establishes fees to cover the cost of providing the service and they must be reasonable and equitable for all. An Advisory Committee was established in 1990 and the following members were appointed: David T. Bateman, John R. Grimes, Stewart Precythe, Reuben E. James, Jerry

Laughter, Graham O'Berry and Russell Roberson. These men represent some of the best minds in agribusiness and have made positive contributions helping set fees and providing sound advice.

Chapter 6

Government And The Farmer

"The punishment suffered by the wise who refuse to take part in the government is to live under the government of bad men."

Plato

No subject, except perhaps the weather, evokes as much emotion among farmers as does talk about government. And as farmers discuss the government, they also cuss it. Like other constituents, farmers tend to blame the government when things don't go their way. And, I suspect, we all tend to expect too much from the government. Some of the criticism may be well founded; however, it should be noted for the record that the government has played a major role in the development of agriculture from the days of manual labor, fish fertilizer, planting by the moon phase and haphazard selection of seeds.

The fact is that government always has played a major role in the farmer's life.

It was an errant farm policy by King George of England that angered the early American colonists into revolting, a declaration of independence and the war that established this country as free and independent. The problem was that English merchants through a policy of high tariffs and taxes placed the colonial planters at a great disadvantage by forcing them to sell their products cheaply to merchants in the Mother Country. Manufactured products were then shipped back to the colonies and sold at high prices. When the American farmers reached their limit of tolerance, that's when they said, "lock and load."

Just over a half century later, a similar conflict resulted from the desire of northern merchants and manufacturers for a steady source of cheap raw products, primarily cotton. The Yankees prevailed in persuading Congress to pass laws that kept the price of cotton low and discouraged its export to more lucrative markets in Europe.

It was this unfair economic/farm policy that placed the Southern planters at such great economic disadvantage and brought them to the brink of secession in 1861.

Ironically, Congress established the U.S. Department of Agriculture, the next year at the urging of President Abraham Lincoln. He called it "the People's Department."

George Washington had proposed the creation of a National Board of Agriculture in 1796. Congress rejected the charm of the Father of our Country and voted down the idea.

The North Carolina General Assembly responded to the plea of Colonel Leonidas Polk who campaigned for more than a decade after he returned from the Civil War, wounded and broke but with a vision of the need for help for the farmer. Polk had been fascinated by the beautiful, green fields he saw in Virginia and believed the same scenes could be repeated on the barren, red clay hills of North Carolina with better knowledge about planting techniques that could be made available to the unlettered farmers by the government.

It was a novel idea which legislators warmed up to slowly. But in the end, in 1877, the North Carolina General Assembly voted to establish the North Carolina Board of Agriculture. The Board moved promptly to enlist the services of Colonel Polk as the State's first Commissioner of Agriculture.

Initially, the role of the Department was to protect farmers from unscrupulous fertilizer dealers and to collect and publish statistics about farm crops. Fertilizer dealers exploited the ignorant farmers and flooded the state with worthless material which they sold as fertilizer. One of the first people hired by Commissioner Polk was a State Chemist whose main job was to test fertilizer and make sure it contained the nutrients which the manufacturers and distributors claimed it contained.

The Department's initial funding came from an assessment of $500 per fertilizer manufacturer. Fertilizer manufacturers contested this assessment all the way to the North Carolina Supreme Court which upheld the legislation and validated the purpose and mission of the Department.

The North Carolina Department of Agriculture found its way slowly during its first century, searching for ways to serve the farmer, to research the mysteries of the soil, seek superior seed and increase knowledge that would increase productivity.

Not until the crisis of the Great Depression when the American way of life experienced its greatest threat did the United States Congress enact a pro-active farm policy designed to stabilize the price of farm crops and create for the farmer a steady market for the fruit of his labor.

Few other state and federal programs work in such harmony as do the farm programs. There are many examples of splendid cooperation between the North Carolina Department of Agriculture and the U.S. Department of Agriculture.

The Proper Role of Government

Much progress has been made in my lifetime in the way crops are grown, harvested and marketed and much of that change can be attributed directly to government programs designed to benefit both the farmer and the consumer. I saw my father cut hay with a hand scythe. He plowed the hard clay soil of Rowan County guiding a walking plow pulled by a team of stubborn mules. The hand scythe and the walking plow are now relics in a museum.

The first role of government at both the state and national levels was to collect information about farming. This information enabled the farmer to learn about his trade and to improve his practices. He learned about seeds, how to save the best of his harvest for the seeds of the next season. He learned about plant nutrient requirements and the need to rotate crops. He learned about the best planting times. From the information which government agencies collected, he learned about successful methods other farmers were using and he imitated them.

The next role of government was to serve as regulator to protect the farmer from unscrupulous operators. For example, much of the fertilizer sold in North Carolina was worthless before the North Carolina Department of Agriculture was created. A major reason the Department was created was to protect the farmer from dishonest merchants and distributors of inferior products.

An Agent of Change

Government became an agent of change beginning with World War I. The country needed large supplies of foodstuffs for its troops in Europe and the government responded by taking a more active role encouraging the farmer to replace the mule with modern machinery. The government also became, for the first time, a major consumer of agricultural products.

During the Great Depression, which began a decade after the end of World War I, government assumed an even larger role in American agriculture. Many of today's government farm program components of production controls, subsidized credit and price supports have their genesis in President Franklin D. Roosevelt's bold initiatives to get the country out of its worst economic crisis ever.

World War II brought even greater and more rapid changes to the American farm. The war created a tremendous demand for farm products. The new era of prosperity stimulated a rapid growth of technology which resulted in mass production of modern tractors, cultivators and ongoing research in developing a vast array of labor saving equipment.

The past fifty years have seen the greatest growth in agricultural technology and a corresponding increase in farm production of any period in the entire history of man. Government has been a major player in this unprecedented era of progress.

Agricultural Policy

The development and implementation of agricultural policy by the federal government has played a major role in the American farm economy for half a century.

What Congress decides to do in the way of price supports, production controls, farm credit and marketing assistance has far reaching impact across the fruited plains.

Government farm policy at the federal level has focused upon three major areas:

1. Increasing efficiency of the farmer and his equipment.
2. Raising and stabilizing farm income.
3. Improving the qualify of life for farmers.

A major goal of the government's agricultural policy is to make sure that population growth does not outpace the food supply. By that measurement, the American farm story is a great success story.

At the beginning of this century, the typical farmer struggled to feed his own family. Mere survival was a prime measure of success at the end of each year. Living conditions were minimal. Primitive homes barely kept out the rain and varmints. There was neither electricity nor indoor plumbing. Infant mortality averaged fifty percent or higher in the backwoods country. One way the farmer sought to overcome these odds was to produce a large family which provided labor for the planting and harvest season and a larger family guaranteed the survival of some offspring.

During the past century, the production of the American farmer has increased to the point where each farmer now produces enough to feed himself and 100 others. Only two percent of the country's population is now engaged in farming and that two percent grows enough food and fiber to feed and clothe the rest of us and provide a large surplus to be exported to other nations of the world.

Increasing Farm Efficiency

Improved technology has changed the farm remarkably over the past century and government has played a significant role in that evolution. In 1862, the federal government created the U.S. Department of Agriculture and that same year, it passed the Land-Grant College Act which led to the establishment of a modern system of land-grant colleges. Our own North Carolina State University had its humble beginnings as a land-grant college and it ranks today as one of the nation's top universities. NC State has pioneered some of the great agricultural research programs in the nation.

In 1914, the U.S. Congress created the Federal Agricultural Extension Service which provided a uniform system of getting the new found knowledge about better agricultural practices directly to the farmer. And in 1917, the federal government appropriated funds for a system of agricultural education in the secondary schools. These new ideas and the money to implement them marked the beginning of a national policy to promote agricultural research and education.

Great strides have been made in agricultural research, in the development of improved seeds, new varieties of crops, better breeds of livestock and greater efficiency in storage and marketing of crops.

Many programs grew from this national policy of increasing farm efficiency. The Production Credit Administration was developed during the Great Depression as a means of providing badly needed capital. The Rural Electrification Administration was created to take electricity to rural America to sparsely populated communities which could not be served profitably by commercial electric companies.

The Federal Soil Conservation Service was created to improve soil conservation measures and re-capture land that had been abandoned because its nutrients were exhausted from poor farming methods.

A great deal of effort went into research aimed at improving the efficiency of farm equipment. The first gasoline powered engines to drive farm equipment were quite primitive by today's standards. By World War I, the mule was being replaced on large farms by tractors. However, it was not until World War II, that the mechanized farm became a reality. More change has taken place on the typical farm in the past half century than occurred in the previous two thousand years. Those of us fortunate enough to have witnessed this great era of progress are indeed among the blessed people.

Raising and Stabilizing Farm Income

The second major goal of our national and state farm policy, has been to raise and stabilize farm income. The typical farmer today still does not earn as much money as his peer in industry; however, he makes a good living and thanks to a number of federal programs his income is fairly well stabilized.

This has been achieved through price supports for farm products, production controls, subsidies, tariffs and storage programs.

In North Carolina the tobacco stabilization program which limits the amount of tobacco grown and then provides a minimum price for the harvested product is the best example of how farm policy has benefitted the individual farmer.

The federal crop insurance program, designed to stabilize farm income against losses from bad weather, is another example of how the government has intervened on behalf of the farmer.

The typical farmer had very little cash income at the turn of the century. He grew most of what he needed on the farm and he traded his surplus of poultry, pork or grain for the few things he could not grow, such as sugar, spices and even store bought clothes.

It was not unusual for the early farmer to pay his lawyer in chickens and pigs for the few times he needed legal advice. While that method of trade and barter may sound romantic today, it represented a harsh and brutal existence which the farmer who lived that way of life was happy to exchange for a system that put cash in his pockets.

In recent years, efforts to raise and stabilize farm income have dominated government programs and have been at the forefront of our national debates about farm policy.

Improved Quality of Life

The ultimate objective of all farm policy has been and continues to be the improved quality of life not only for the country's farmers but also a better way of life for all citizens. The fact that has been achieved is abundantly evident.

An adequate supply of food and fiber, available at a reasonable price, benefits all citizens. The farmer benefits by having a stable market for his products. The consumer benefits by having a steady supply of safe and affordable food.

The dairy farmer is better off by being able to count on a steady market for his milk at $1 a gallon rather than the occasional opportunity to sell his milk at $10 a gallon but then not able to sell any milk at all some of the time.

There are many indicators that the quality of life has improved for both the farmer and the consumer. You can see the evidence of prosperity as you drive through our rural country. Brand new pickup trucks are parked in front of pretty homes, beautifully landscaped with flowers and shrubs. Farmers send their children to the universities in pursuit of an even better life for the next generation.

Supply and Demand

A major and appropriate role of government farm policy is to alleviate the hardships created by the basic law of supply and demand which once dealt the farmer some of his most brutal defeats. Due to the seasonality of farming and the relatively short growing season for most crops, farmers when left to their own devices would face large price fluctuations. Take apple growers, for example. Without the marketing, storage and distribution programs in place now, apple growers would see a rapid decrease in the price of apples during the peak of apple harvest when there is an abundant supply of apples. In the middle of the winter, however, when there are no apples to be bought, the theoretical price of apples would sky rocket, but of no value to the apple farmer because he had no apples to sell. That was the problem which farmers faced in the Great Depression. Farm prices fluctuated constantly and wildly, like a great roller coaster.

Off season prices soared widely when products were scarce. But during harvest times of plenty, prices plummeted to the point where farmers had to sell their produce below what it cost them to grow their crops. In turn, the farmers could not pay for supplies and equipment. Many farmers lost their land.

By structuring programs to mitigate the effects of wide fluctuations in supply and demand upon the farmer, government has played a major role in helping the farmer to avoid many of his most troublesome problems.

Government: Its Proper Role

To be sure, the government has played a major role in the life of the farmer, both at the state and national levels. It should be noted that the government's involvement in farm policy always has been at the request of the farmer to help relieve his misery in times of great crisis.

The Civil War was the first great farm crisis which resulted in the establishment of the U.S. Department of Agriculture and the system of Land Grant Colleges which have meant so much to agricultural progress.

Most of the government programs we enjoy today had their genesis in the Great Depression when farmers could not sell their products even for a fraction of what it cost to produce them. The federal government has led the way in gathering important information about crops, marketing conditions, scientific methods of planting, developing improved seed, technology advancement and developing foreign markets for the American farmer.

We at the state level have sought to serve our local constituency in ways that are relevant and appropriate. It would be a reasonable assertion and conclusion to say that the government, certainly as this statement pertains to the North Carolina Department of Agriculture, has been a partner to the farmer.

We have stood by the farmer in his time of need, seeking to alleviate his misery caused by drought, floods, ravenous insects and other perils beyond his ability to cope with them. We have sought, with his consent, better methods of planting and harvesting crops so that his output would be increased. And, we have sought to assure the customer that our farm products are safe and consistent with what they are supposed to be.

I am confident that, at least in North Carolina, the farmer is much better off than he would have been without the government taking such an active role in looking out for his welfare. We have done that because it is in the interest of all our citizens that the farmer succeeds.

In the end, we do not eat until the farmer's work is done.

Chapter 7

Major Cash Crops

Tobacco: The First Crop

"Tobacco is divine, there is nothing to equal it."
Pierre Corneille, 1673

I make no apology for tobacco. It was North Carolina's first money crop. Tobacco has been the foundation of North Carolina agriculture for more than two centuries.

Just three decades ago, tobacco accounted for nearly half of all of the state's cash farm income. Today, tobacco sales total just over $1 billion annually and account for only about 15 per cent of the total farm cash income.

Only in the past decade has the cash income from tobacco not been the leading source of cash income for North Carolina farmers.

"It has been truly said," historian Hugh Lefler wrote, "the North Carolina tobacco crop was worth more that all the wheat in Kansas, or all the pigs in Iowa, or all the cotton in Mississippi."[28]

I am proud that we've diversified North Carolina agriculture to the point where we no longer depend upon a single source for most of our cash income. However, we should never forget the role that tobacco played in getting us to this point. To be sure, we should be mindful of any real health threats which may result from the misuse of this product and we should take stern measures to prevent the use of tobacco and many other products by minors. I will defend tobacco to the day of my departure from this office and from this planet.

Tobacco has become, in the past few years, a controversial crop. The controversy stems from what some say are harmful

[28] Lelfer, p. 611.

health effects caused by excessive use of tobacco. I will leave that debate to the medical experts. Crisis is no stranger to North Carolina's tobacco farmers. I can recall some type of tobacco crisis every year during my three decades as Commissioner of Agriculture. The threats have ranged from natural perils such as adverse weather--drought, hail, hurricane force winds--to human hazards such as higher taxes, increased government regulation and litigation.

Each year, it seems that the risks facing tobacco get greater and greater. And now, as this book is being written, we face our greatest two-pronged threat---life and death regulation by the federal Food and Drug Administration and a pending legal settlement which I believe will sound the death toll for the tobacco program in this country as we know it now. However, I am convinced that tobacco will always be grown in North Carolina, in parts of the United States and around the world.

No one can dispute the many beneficial economic contributions which tobacco has brought us. For more than 200 years, tobacco has been the leading source of farm income in North Carolina.

Tobacco money enabled the farmer to live from one season to the next. Tobacco money clothed the farmer's family, sent his children to school and enabled him to purchase modern equipment to mechanize the farm.

Tobacco money built Duke University and Wake Forest University and their two great world class medical schools. Tobacco money has provided millions of dollars for agricultural research.

Until recently, many of those who currently attack tobacco were among its staunchest supporters. I am referring, of course, to the newspaper editors and television commentators who, as long as their newspapers and television stations benefitted from tobacco advertising dollars, were supportive of North Carolina's leading crop. Only when tobacco advertising dollars were no longer coming their way did the newspaper editors and television commentators muster the courage to criticize tobacco. I find that a bit cynical.

The demise of tobacco will have a far reaching and adverse impact upon our economy. In addition to the significant direct impact, in terms of jobs and personal income which tobacco brings to communities throughout the state, there is a very important secondary impact to consider. Take, for example, the hundreds millions of dollars in state and local taxes generated by tobacco.

Without tobacco, the land on which it now grows would become less valuable and produce less in property taxes for county and municipal governments. I doubt very seriously if those who would destroy tobacco have thought of the many other good things they will destroy with it.

Year	Acres	Yield lb /acre	Production 1,000 lbs	Value $1,000	Av Price
1940	843,000	964	812,540	$ 123,893	15.20
1950	640,000	1,441	858,140	477,508	55.60
1960	457,000	1,836	839,870	512,731	61.10
1970	383,800	2,076	796,941	571,211	71.70
1980	374,000	1,991	744,765	1,089,452	146.3
1990	276,000	2,252	621,640	1,044,398	168.1
1994	235,000	2,477	582,035	992,480	170.5

North Carolina Flue-cured Tobacco Crops 1940-1994
Table 8

A Brief History of Tobacco

Tobacco is an original product of America. The natives of South America, particularly the shaman (medicine doctors) used tobacco for ceremonial and medicinal purposes as far back as 8,000 years ago.

Early explorers came to this continent in search of gold and other precious metals. A Spanish explorer openly searched for the fountain of youth. They did not find gold, nor did they find a magical antidote to old age. What they did find, however, was a future source of gold in the green plant which they had witnessed the natives using in a rather strange fashion.

Sir Walter Raleigh, the favorite advisor to Queen Elizabeth who had argued so persuasively for an English colony here, quickly became Europe's first great fan of tobacco. There is a legend that Sir Raleigh's manservant was so shocked to find his lord emitting smoke from his nose and mouth that he doused the knight with a pail of ale.

Shortly after the discovery of the recreational aspects of tobacco in the mid-1580s, the English tried to grow their own crop. However, neither the soil nor climate was suitable for growing tobacco which remained in the domain of the new world. About the same time, Spain began to import a high quality and smokable brand from its colony in the West Indies and by the 1590s choice tobacco was selling in Europe for as much as $125 per pound. Inferior tobacco brought $15 a pound. Such prices created a great demand for the product and its fame spread quickly.

The first English settlement in the new world, at Manteo in Dare County, failed. Hence the first permanent English settlement later at Jamestown, Virginia. Virginia planters got a head start in clearing their virgin forests, planting tobacco and developing a lucrative market for their coveted crop.

As the settlement spread south into the Albemarle area, which is now the northeastern corner of North Carolina, Tar Heel farmers quickly made tobacco their principal crop, after producing the necessary foodstuffs.

The value of tobacco was so universally accepted that it became a form of money. Lawyers, preachers, school teachers and even soldiers were paid for their services in tobacco which they in turn traded for goods and services they needed.

A brisk trade in tobacco developed, shipped first through the Virginia port and then from a North Carolina port at Edenton. The British Parliament validated the value of tobacco by taxing it. In 1660, Parliament passed the Navigation Act which required that all commodities from the colonies be shipped first to a British port where the duties would be collected. In 1673, the Parliamentary

Plantation Act assessed a penny a pound tax on tobacco, even when it was sent from one colony to another.

Farmers and traders then began to devote a certain amount of ingenuity and effort to evading the taxes as they continued to improve the quality of their leaf.

William Byrd, the surveyor who kept a prolific journal of his observations along the Virginia-North Carolina border, wrote of the tobacco trade, "The Trade hither is engrosst by the Saints of New England, who carry off a great deal of Tobacco, without troubling themselves with paying that Impertinent Duty of a Penny a Pound."

North Carolina farmers rebelled against the tobacco tax in 1673 in a violent episode which became known as Culpepper's Rebellion. John Culpepper was declared governor by the rebels and the tax collector sent from England to collect the tax fled back to England, afraid for his life.

The English Lords replaced Culpepper and patiently waited for resentment against the tax to abate.

Colonial tobacco was cut down whole and sun-dried much in the fashion that burley tobacco is cured today. Leaves were then stripped from the stalks and packed into hogsheads weighing about 1,000 pounds. They were dragged to market by horses and mules or rolled by the farmers over rough paths which became known as "rolling roads."

By the mid-1700s, tobacco had become such a prominent crop that the General Assembly enacted an inspection act which led to a uniform set of standards for grading the product.

North Carolina was not the dominant tobacco state we are today. As recent as 1840, Virginia planters annually produced four times (120 million pounds) as much tobacco as did North Carolina farmers (30 million pounds). But that was before the discovery of "bright leaf."

Bright Leaf

Early smokers loved their tobacco strong and pungent. However, after a century of smoking, a new generation began to demand a milder flavor. Farmers were encouraged to experiment with planting in new soils, cross breeding different types of tobacco and trying new curing methods.

Tobacco promoters knew what they wanted long before they achieved it. They tried for years to develop a thin, yellowish leaf which could be dried or cured to a bright golden hue. This process, they rightfully concluded, would produce a tobacco that would yield a mild and delightful aromatic flavor. They would call this process, when it eventually came into full bloom, "Bright Leaf."

By accident, a young slave in Caswell County discovered the process by which "Bright Leaf" tobacco came to be produced. Stephen, a blacksmith on the farm of Captain Abisha Slade fell asleep while tending wood fires on the floor of the curing barn. While he napped, the fires nearly went out. When he awakened and discovered his plight, he went to a nearby pit where charcoal logs were smoldering and threw the hot coals on the dying barn-floor fire. The heat came up quickly. In a short while, the drying leaves became a sparkling bright-yellow, a rich color never seen in cured tobacco.

Captain Slade's first "Bright Leaf" brought four times the average price for other tobacco when he sold it in the fall of 1839 at the nearby Danville, Virginia, tobacco market. He eagerly shared the secret of how this desirable golden leaf had been developed and other farmers began to imitate his process.

In the absence of a centralized program to take charge of the research and exploit Stephen's discovery, it took two full decades before an efficient method of duplicating the result with open fires. And it was not until the 1870s that a closed furnace inside the barn came into use.

It was also about this time that fertilizers had been developed to replenish the poor, worn out sandy soils most suitable for growing tobacco. The advent of Bright Leaf tobacco, along with the development of fertilizers, restored value to farm lands which had been abandoned for years. It had been the practice for more than a century to clear a tract of land, plant it in tobacco for a few years until the natural nutrients were used up and then abandon the tract and move on to a new field to be cleared and planted.

With the arrival of Bright Leaf tobacco in the Piedmont and coastal regions of the state, worthless farm land suddenly became very valuable property.

The Civil War was both a curse and a blessing to the North Carolina farmer and his fledgling cash crop. Farming just about came to a halt during the war because most of the able bodied men were conscripted into the Confederate Army. Wives and children managed to grow food for the table and little else.

Bull Durham Discovered

The war did produce a great demand for North Carolina tobacco. At the end of the war, in fact as leaders of the opposing armies were meeting to discuss terms for surrender and peace, soldiers stumbled onto the little tobacco factory and shop of John Ruffin Green at Durham's Station. Green had developed quite a market for his product among the students of the nearby University of North Carolina.

Soldiers, not in a buying mood, sampled Green's tobacco until it was all gone. Fortunately for him, they did not bother his manufacturing equipment and they left him a single pouch for his own enjoyment.

After the war, letters began to arrive at Durham's Station, addressed variously to the mayor (there wasn't one), the police chief (not one either) and the railroad baggage master. The correspondents inquired as to how they could obtain a subsequent supply of the fine tobacco they had enjoyed and how they would be happy to pay for it. This sequence of events led to one of the first great tobacco marketing stories. Mr. Green began to call his product "Bull Durham," and it became world famous as production increased dramatically to keep up with the great demand.

Cigarette Manufacturing

Cigarettes were made by hand until a young Virginian, James A. Bonsack, developed a machine for rolling cigarettes in the early 1880s.

Expert workers could turn out four, or at most five, cigarettes a minute at peak production. While this meant a fast worker could produce 15,000 cigarettes in a 60-hour week, it was still a labor intensive operation.

North Carolina traces its origin as a great tobacco manufacturing state to the decision of an Orange County farmer who returned from the Civil War with nothing more than two blind army mules, symbolic of the devastation of the War, and fifty cents. Washington Duke and his sons grew tobacco on their farm and then peddled it from town to town with the wagon pulled by the blind mules. Cash was scarce everywhere so they traded tobacco for things they could use, flour, cotton, brown sugar and other "luxuries" that did not grow on the farm.

Demand for the tobacco was so great they built a "log factory" to refine their product and then they moved to Durham and built a larger factory.

When Washington Duke installed Mr. Bonsack's machine in his burgeoning cigarette factory in Durham in 1884, it was soon producing 120,000 cigarettes a day. It was the beginning of automation and a new era for manufacturing and for the economy of North Carolina.

The following year after Duke automated his plant, cigarette manufacturers recorded their accumulative production of the first billion. Duke's factory was not the first, nor the biggest; however, it became the fastest growing, due to the diligent efforts of his son, James Buchanan (Buck) Duke, who started with nothing and built the American Tobacco Company into the world's largest tobacco manufacturing and marketing consortium.

Buck Duke had a vision for business and a genius for recruiting the best men to manage his operations. His rise from "rags-to-riches" became one of the great American success stories that rivaled the achievements of his contemporaries--Henry Ford, Andrew Carnegie and Harvey Firestone.

Richard Joshua Reynolds established his manufacturing plant in Winston-Salem and the race was on in North Carolina to make the most and the best tobacco products.

In the process of becoming the biggest and best tobacco manufacturer, Duke swallowed the Reynolds company and all the other companies only to have his conglomerate attacked as a monopoly and broken up by the U.S. Department of Justice and the U.S. Supreme Court.

North Carolina farmers benefitted immensely from the vision and success of Buck Duke because of the rapid growth in demand for good tobacco and for the steady prices.

By the end of the 19th Century, North Carolina farmers had overtaken their Virginia counterparts and had become the nation's leading tobacco producers. The availability of good tobacco gave impetus to the manufacturers to expand. Intense competition among the manufacturers created a strong market for tobacco farmers.

In 1900, the value of tobacco manufactured in North Carolina was estimated at $16 million. A half century later that value had swelled to $1.3 billion.

Today the value of tobacco manufactured in North Carolina exceeds $11 billion annually. Tobacco is one of the great tax producers in the country. Nationwide, federal taxes collected from the sale of tobacco totaled more than $5.6 billion last year and state excise taxes brought in another $6.7 billion revenue.

On top of this, 450 cities and towns and counties impose cigarette taxes ranging from one cent to 25 cents per pack. These local taxes produce nearly $200 million revenue annually for the local governments that charge the tax.

Advanced farm practices increased the yield in 1994 to 2,477 pounds of flue-cured tobacco per acre. This was 159 pounds per acre above the previous high yield recorded in 1991.

The 1982 remains the high water mark for the most cash income from flue-cured tobacco in North Carolina when growers received a record $1.2 billion for the 756,305 pounds produced. Since that time quotas have been steadily reduced to where only 582,000 pounds of tobacco were produced in 1994 and that brought $992 million.

North Carolina produces three-fifths of all the flue-cured tobacco sold in the United States.

Conclusion

Tobacco has brought great wealth and social progress to North Carolina. The memories of men like R. J. Reynolds and Washington Duke linger on in the benevolent legacies of Wake

Forest University and Bowman Gray School of Medicine; Duke University and Duke Medical Center. Duke Power Company originated from the generosity of Buck Duke who returned to his native North Carolina at the end of his tobacco days and invested millions of dollars harnessing the latent power of the Catawba and other Piedmont rivers. Thousands of students from North Carolina and the rest of the nation have benefitted from scholarships funded by tobacco money. Endowments to church organizations, minority institutions, children's homes and numerous other educational and social agencies have been enriched by the success of tobacco.

I would suggest those who attack tobacco consider the good it has done for millions of North Carolinians who traveled this path before them and whose lives were enriched immeasurably by the many beneficial aspects of tobacco.

Cotton Makes a Comeback

Cotton has been a crop of peril for the North Carolina farmer. When times were good for growing and selling cotton, they were very good but there were many bad times as well. The price of cotton has fluctuated drastically, rising to a high of 88 cents a pound during the Civil War and dropping to a low of a nickel a pound in the 1890s and again during the Great Depression. Weather and the boll weevil wreaked their own havoc with the cotton crop. The politics of cotton have long been attributed as a factor in the war between the North and the South.

Cotton became an important crop in the South just before the Civil War. It was grown chiefly on the large plantations of the deep South, cultivated by slaves. Historians blame much of the animosity that developed between the North and the South in the first half of the 19th century on the cotton culture.

There has been a strong demand for cotton for more than 200 years because of its value in producing a soft, comfortable cloth. The development of mechanical weaving devices for manufacturing raw cotton into cloth in the mid-1700s and the invention of the cotton gin in 1793 by Eli Whitney greatly accelerated the demand for cotton in the 1800s.

The North, characterized by its long winters and relatively short growing season was not a suitable climate for growing cotton.

However, northern capitalists and merchants controlled both the manufacture and the domestic market for raw cotton. They dominated the national congress which enacted laws restricting the free trade of cotton to the lucrative markets in Europe.

In the absence of any government protection, southern planters were vulnerable to the influence and whims of the northern mercantile class. It was cotton, more than any other single crop which perpetuated the evil of slavery into the mid-19th Century.

Except for a few large planters in eastern North Carolina, cotton was largely a crop of misery for most North Carolina farmers who attempted to grow it. The price of cotton fluctuated from a high of 25 cents a pound in 1868 to less than a nickel a pound in 1894.

There was only one cotton mill which manufactured raw cotton into cloth in North Carolina in 1815 and only 39 such mills in 1860, at the outbreak of the Civil War. North Carolina benefitted from the rapid transition of textile mills from the northeast to the southeast as six new textile mills opened each year. By 1900 there were some 170 mills in operation. And while the pay averaged only $200 a year, that was hard cash and it was more money than could be sprouted from the typical farm. Thousands of farmers left the land for industrial jobs.

Cotton production expanded sharply during the first quarter of this century; however, it was at huge cost in sweat, toil and tears. Between 1900 and 1925, cotton production in North Carolina increased from 460,000 bales a year to 1.1 million bales. However, the price of cotton fluctuated between 10 cents and a nickel a pound while it cost the farmer an average seven cents a pound to grow a crop.

The prevalent method of farming from the end of the Civil War in 1865 until the Great Depression in 1933 was tenant farming, which next to slavery must go down as the most evil cloud to hang over the good North Carolina soil. After the Civil War, most of the large plantations were broken into smaller tracts and tended by share-croppers or tenant farmers. In principal, the concept of tenant farming sounded fine. Landless farmers, primarily poor whites and blacks, depended on the system for a place to survive. In reality, tenant farming was little more than a poorly disguised form of economic bondage.

Under the practices of tenant farming, a farmer with no cash was provided foodstuffs and clothing for his family and seed and fertilizer for his crop on credit by a merchant who held a lien on the farmer's crop for payment. The merchant charged the farmer a premium for the things he bought on credit; however, the farmer usually got the lowest price for his crop

In addition, the farmer was charged excessively high interest rates of 30 and 40 percent. More often than not, the farmer ended up deeper in debt each year. The merchant insisted that the farmer grow more and more of the cash crop, usually cotton, to raise money to pay his debt. This left little time or land for raising food.

Farm tenancy was credited with producing a major deficit of vegetables, livestock and feed crops during the 1920s. The 1925 Census of Agriculture revealed that out of 283,000 farms more than half had no hogs, no cows, no hay or forage, no Irish potatoes nor any sweet potatoes. More than three-fourths of the farms had no beef cattle. These products, when they could be afforded at all, had to be imported from other states at exorbitant prices.

"The greatest curse of the agricultural South is our vicious time-prices credit system," wrote editor Clarence Poe of Raleigh, in the *Progressive Farmer*, January 19, 1929. "It is a curse alike to landowners, tenants, merchants, bankers, professional men, and to county and state as units of government. It is holding our whole section back just as truly as it was forty years ago when that great southern orator, Henry W. Grady, portrayed its blighting influence on our section and gave his eloquent and stirring prophecy of a better day: -- 'When every farmer in the South shall eat bread from his own fields and meat from his own pastures and be disturbed by no creditors and enslaved by no debt, shall sit amid his teeming gardens, and orchards, and vineyards, and dairies, and barnyards, pitching his crops to his own wisdom and growing them in independence, making cotton his clean surplus, and selling it in his own time, and in his chosen market, and not at a master's bidding, getting his pay in cash and not in a receipted mortgage that discharges his debt but does not restore his freedom, then shall he break the fullness of our day.'"

Chapter 8

The Good Farmer Is A Steward of The Land

We Must Live in Harmony With the Good Earth, the Land, Air, and Water, Else We Will Destroy the Very Resources That Sustain Life for Us and Our Posterity.

I have been always a strong advocate for the farmer. That is my job. But also, I have always been a strong advocate of protecting the land. That is the legacy of my father who was one of the earliest and most enthusiastic champions of soil conservation. More than anything else my father taught me, I remember his admonition almost daily, "Jim, take care of the soil and it will take care of you."

A major goal of mine in the past 33 years as Commissioner has been to keep our farmers in the front in adopting new technologies that would improve their production and livelihood while at the same time maintaining their historical roots to the land. As we developed larger, heavier equipment to work the land faster and more economically, we also found we could leave more residue on the land and plow less often (conservation tillage) so that we decreased soil erosion and improved the sustainability of our cropland. With the development of new and highly potent chemicals, we found we could use these more judiciously as species-specific pesticides using smaller amounts and do less harm to our beneficial insects (integrated pest management).

I am proud to have had a role in developing an Agronomic Services Division that provides free soil analysis for our farmers and homeowners so that they in turn can know exactly how much fertilizer to apply to their crops and lawns for both optimum production and optimum environmental protection. I was especially proud to cut the ribbon for our Center for Environmental Farming Systems where research and demonstration/education efforts will focus on the development of farming systems that are environmental, economically and socially sustainable. Farming has changed dramatically over the past 33 years but we have never lost sight of the need to guarantee that future generations will find productive lands and clean waters to sustain their basic needs for food and fiber.

Nearly a quarter of a century ago, I spoke to a legislative committee which was then considering the problem of animal waste and I suggested to North Carolina's lawmakers that they find a balanced solution to the problem. That strategy made sense then and it makes sense today.

Here is a statement I made to the General Assembly's Legislative Research Commission's Subcommittee on Animal Waste, May 12, 1972:

> "The disposal of animal waste has become a real concern of all our citizens--consumers and producers alike.
>
> "It is a problem for our consumers in that its solution will be an expense to be added to the cost of food.
>
> "It is a concern for our farmers not only as to how to eliminate the problems of animal waste disposal but that of how to protect their businesses from urban sprawl that is evident wherever you look.
>
> "From the beginning of time, there has been pollution of our streams and lands. If you will look back only a few years to the great buffalo herds that roamed the plains and polluted our rivers and streams to a degree that is not now prevalent, you can get a truer picture of the pollution problems which we now face with confinement feeding.
>
> "Farmers have always used animal waste as a means of fertilizing their fields and will continue as this offers the best potential with the least

> pollution of our river systems. Let me stress that we recognize the dangers of excessive pollution of our rivers but also let me point out that we must maintain some semblance of balance in consideration of problems associated with pollution."

There has been a grandiose scheme by the media, by some politicians and by others who have contributed significantly to river pollution to blame much, if not all the problems of our dying rivers upon our farmers. That is not fair and it is not true.

To be sure, farmers are a part of the problem and we must solve the problems we create. We are working hard to do that. However, it would be a great mistake to assume that hog farmers are even the major culprits in destroying the Neuse River, which serves as the best example of how such an important part of our environment is sacrificed in the name of prosperity.

When I first moved to Raleigh in the mid-50s, long before hog farming became a major activity, the Neuse River was well on its way toward becoming a public sewer. That was because the growing towns of Durham and Raleigh found the river to be the cheapest and most convenient place to dispose of their human waste.

The story of Raleigh's reluctance to be a good citizen is a well-documented tale, recorded in the annals of the North Carolina Supreme Court which found it necessary more than 60 years ago to order the officials of our Capital City to do what the law already commanded them to do and what good men would have done out of the goodness of their hearts.

Raleigh's Poor Example

Just over one hundred years ago the city of Raleigh built a sewage treatment plant which didn't treat the sewage of the Capital City but rather pumped it through two pipes, one in Walnut Creek and the other in Crabtree Creek, both of which emptied a short distance away into the Neuse River. Raleigh saw no problem with this method of disposing of their foul feces.

Thirty-three miles downstream the poor people of Smithfield saw a real problem. For Smithfield officials pleaded with their neighbors to the north to stop polluting the Neuse River which was then, as now, the town's sole source of drinking water. Knowing that they were in violation of a state law that prohibited dumping raw sewage into a stream or river, Raleigh city officials thumbed their noses at the law and their neighbors downstream. "Sue us and we'll see you in court," was their arrogant response.

That's just what the town of Smithfield did. In 1934, Raleigh was hauled kicking and screaming into the Superior Court of North Carolina. This case is aptly documented in Volume 207 of "North Carolina Reports," pages 597-600.

Raleigh admitted it was doing what it was accused of doing and Raleigh city officials knew their sewage treatment policy was in direct violation of state law (G.S. 7125). However, Raleigh argued that it simply could not afford to build a sewage treatment plant as required by the law. Furthermore, pleaded the defendants "if the city of Raleigh were restrained from using its sewage system... untold misery and suffering would be entailed upon a population of over 40,000 people."

The Raleigh city fathers tried to bolster their case by pointing out to the court that in addition to handling the sewage of the good citizens, Raleigh also dumped into the Neuse River the raw sewage from State College, State Prison, Central Hospital for the Insane, the Institution for the Blind, the State Capitol, Governor's Mansion, all State Departments, Peace Institute, St. Mary's College and various suburban developments.

The presiding judge found as a matter of fact that "There was no evidence that Smithfield has suffered inconvenience by reason of the defendant's violation of G.S. 7125 and there was no evidence of a single case of typhoid fever, colitis, dysentery or any other disease caused by pathogenic bacteria."

In perhaps the strangest finding of the case, the judge concluded that since the "population of Smithfield was only 6.81 percent of the population which would be affected by the decree prayed for," it didn't seem quite fair to force Raleigh to do what the law required them to do--stop polluting the Neuse River.

In ruling against the Smithfield plaintiffs, Superior Court Judge Henry A. Grady of Clinton found their case without merit. He added insult to their injury by ordering them to pay the costs of the defendants.

Explaining his logic, Judge Grady wrote in his decision, "The court has drunk of its water and bathed in it and has suffered no ill effects therefrom."

The North Carolina Supreme Court quickly overturned Grady's decision with a harsh rebuke. "The ancient mode of 'trial by water' was aforetime deemed efficacious in determining the guilt or innocence of witches and by applying the practices of the ancient law the distinguished jurist has found the waters of Neuse River not guilty."

The state Supreme Court ordered the City of Raleigh to comply with the law that said they could not dump raw sewage into the Neuse or any other river. That decision was handed down in 1935, some sixty one years ago. It took the city fathers nearly three decades to build a modern sewage plant and when that facility finally opened for business in the mid-1960s, it was already too small to handle the city's flood of human waste.

The point I'm trying to make is that the city of Raleigh has not operated an adequate sewage treatment plant for much of the past century. The consequence of this neglect has been and continues to be the frequent dumping of hundreds of millions of gallons of harmful sewage into the Neuse River.

In September of 1996, the day after Hurricane Fran paid an eventful visit through central North Carolina, Raleigh's sewage plant was shut down during a power failure and more than 125 million gallons of raw sewage was pumped directly into the Neuse River. There was a similar discharge the following day. The devastation of this horrible action was felt for days and weeks down streams as people were forced from their homes, flooded with this sea of human waste and as evidenced by decaying vegetation throughout the flood plain of the Lower Neuse River basin.

This 250-million-gallon spill of Raleigh's raw sewage was documented a few days later in the News and Observer by a small inside story. In 1995, the Raleigh *News and Observer* ran a series of stories documenting the phenomenal growth of North Carolina hog producers and that a few of these producers had neglected to take the proper precautions against harmful waste spills. The largest of these spills was a truly unpardonable 25-million gallon monstrosity. We are struggling to prevent such an event from occurring again.

The *News and Observer* won a Pulitzer Prize for this series of stories and I commend them for that honor. However, even as they were documenting the infrequent spills of hog waste, millions of gallons of raw sewage were flowing routinely from the state's inadequate municipal waste treatment plants into North Carolina's streams and rivers with hardly a mention in the press and not so much as a disapproving frown from the public officials charged with protecting our streams and rivers.

In fact, there has been for sometime an average of at least one municipal spill a day, some of them exceeding a million gallons. Until the late 1990s, none of the state's major newspapers considered these spills newsworthy enough to report. Seldom, has any municipal facility been fined for a sewage spill, no matter how large.

To be sure, hog waste is harmful and should not be allowed to pollute our streams and rivers that provide most North Carolinians with their drinking water. However, untreated municipal sewage is even a greater threat to human health than animal waste. Municipal sewage contains, in addition to human waste, toxic industrial chemicals such as by products from battery acid, mercury, printer's ink and numerous other acrid agents. In addition, municipal sewage includes hospital wastes such as harmful blood-borne viruses and diseases. Raw, untreated municipal sewage poses a very serious threat to public drinking supplies and state officials charged with protecting our essential water should not be tolerant of municipal polluters.

The Division of Water Quality of the Department of Environment, Health and Natural Resources (DEHNR), the state agency charged with enforcing clean water standards, has a staff of 250 people, larger than the entire State Treasurer's Department, yet it has failed time after time, year after year, to take action whenever a major municipal spill occurred. More often than not DEHNR officials apologize for the municipal offenses rather than take the appropriate steps to force the cities to stop dumping millions of gallons of raw sewage illegally.

In the aftermath of Raleigh's 250-million gallon spill of raw sewage into the Neuse River following Hurricane Fran, which devastated vegetation and homes as far as one hundred miles to the South, Capital City officials were remarkably quiet. They never had the courtesy even to say they were sorry, implying the Neuse is there to serve as Raleigh's public sewer whenever needed. DEHNR officials explained the incident as "unavoidable."

The question that comes to my mind is why is a 25 million-gallon spill of hog waste worth a Pulitzer Prize and a 250-million gallon spill of raw municipal sewage worth hardly a mention in the same newspaper?

Growth Is the Real Villain

The real villain is growth. We have become so enamored with promoting growth that we have come to accept the consequences of a new industrial facility as necessary to sustaining the quality of life we have come to enjoy. We have become immune to the problems of industrial pollution because we have been led to believe that the value of new jobs created by new industry exceeds the costs they bring. Perhaps that was so decades ago as we made the transition from an agrarian society to one based on commerce and industry. However, it is past due time that we stopped this incessant march that will eventually take us over a cliff into an abyss of unsolvable problems.

The mere suggestion that we factor into the discussion of economic growth the associated environmental costs is met with violent opposition. I suggest it is time we open up the debate and invite all of those who have helped pollute the Neuse to step to the table and discuss how they are going to remedy the problem.

Let's begin with the city of Raleigh which dumps some 10 billion gallons of treated sewage with a high nitrogen content into the Neuse River each year. That is about one-fourth of the some 40 billion gallons of municipal, residential and industrial treated waste discharged into the Neuse each year by the holders of more than 200 point waste dischargers.

These figures do not include the numerous times each year when malfunctions occur in waste treatment plants and raw sewage is dumped directly into the river, such as in September of 1996 when Raleigh dumped a quarter of a billion gallons untreated waste into the river. In the wake of this great tragedy not even a modest apology was forthcoming to the million citizens downstream for the misery and suffering they endured. You might conclude that Raleigh has come to believe the river is there for its convenience and if that is not agreeable to the people downstream, they ought to move somewhere else or just deal with the adversity the best way they can.

I would suggest that the villain which killed the Neuse River and is in the process of destroying the state's other waterways is not the farmer but those who have blindly promoted growth at the expense of the environment.

North Carolina's population has doubled in recent years and most of that growth has been concentrated in the Piedmont Crescent between Raleigh, along the Interstate-85 corridor which includes Durham, Burlington, Greensboro, High Point, Lexington, Salisbury, Charlotte and Gastonia.

According to the 1990 Census, "roughly half of the households in North Carolina use septic systems or cesspools," Official records document that over 1.4 million septic systems are "in use" in the state and many tens of thousands have been abandoned and remain in the ground as potential ground water pollution sites. The Raleigh *News and Observer* recognized the concern in 1996 and noted that by the year 2000 more than 80 percent of the existing septic tanks will be "prone to frequent failures and leakage." The Winston-Salem *Journal* reported of communities in which health problems are evident as a result of the "failure of up to 85 percent of the town's septic tanks" for more than 30 years."

It comes as no great surprise that the rivers which cascade through these cities bustling with new economic activity are filled with the ugly evidence of modern life--treated and untreated sewage, industrial waste, polluted run-off from over-fertilized yards, golf courses and hundreds of other debris.

In addition to the rapid development inside the cities, hundreds of subdivisions, many of them with inadequate sewage treatment plants have been allowed to dot the banks of our streams and discharge waste directly into the rivers.

Automobiles Pollute, Too

We must not forget the owners of automobiles in our attempt to solve this problem. Environmental engineers tell us that each time a car speeds along a highway it emits a certain amount of nitrogen that settles to the ground and is eventually swept away by the next rainfall to the nearest creek or tributary. There is no proposal in the current pollution abatement plan to curb the pollution created by automobiles.

When the proposed plan to clean up the Neuse River was first released by the Division of Environmental Management, it suggested that farmers were responsible for 60 percent of the excess nitrogen being placed in the Neuse River. I knew then and we all know now that simply isn't true. As a result of that erroneous assumption, the proposal placed an unfair burden on the farmer to clean up the Neuse River.

I am not defending the hog operator responsible for the 25 million gallon spill. Neither should we allow the city of Raleigh to avoid its responsibility for dumping 250 million gallons of untreated human waste into the Neuse. What we should do, however, is to examine the problem completely and fairly. We should adequately identify the problem on the basis of the fact already in hand. There is no need for any additional study. Then we should sit down calmly and firmly and develop a plan that offers a fair solution.

It has been estimated that cleaning up the Neuse River will cost $1 billion or more. If that is the cost, so be it. It is a reasonable price we ought to pay so that our children can enjoy the heritage that once belonged to their ancestors. We should commit ourselves immediately to not only stopping the pollution of the Neuse but also every other river in North Carolina. We should begin the process of reversing the damage to restore our rivers to their pristine state. If that results in a moratorium on growth, it is a fair price to pay. However, everyone should pay the price equally. Farmers should pay their fair share but also should commercial and residential builders, highway contractors, realtors and all who have contributed to the problem of deprecating our environment.

However, the cost should be borne fairly among those who created the problem. The taxpayers of Raleigh, and other cities along the river, the developers of inadequate residential and industrial facilities, and the farmers should pay their fair share. Together we can solve this program and restore a safe, clean and once beautiful river to its original state.

The power to solve this problem rests with the members of the General Assembly who can act whenever they choose to do so. I urged them to consider such a measure in 1972 and I renew that request now.

It is my sincere belief that the good farmer is a steward of the land because his livelihood and his very survival depends on the ability of the land to sustain himself and his family. I have remembered the wise example of my own father who taught me to preserve the soil. It was a lesson of love but more than that, it was a lesson in survival. The farmer, more than anyone else, must be a good steward of the soil, if he is to prevail.

That advice also applies to our rivers and to the water we drink.

I love My Job

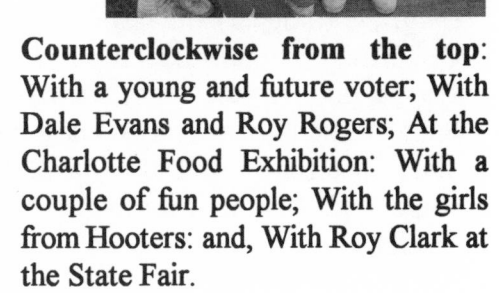

Counterclockwise from the top: With a young and future voter; With Dale Evans and Roy Rogers; At the Charlotte Food Exhibition: With a couple of fun people; With the girls from Hooters: and, With Roy Clark at the State Fair.

TOP: With a special friend, and Hargrove (Skipper) Bowles in 1972. CENTER: At the Ramp Festival in Waynesville, as Zeb Alley watches; Eating "Chitluns with Secretary of State Thad Eure. RIGHT: With Bob Hope and Charlie Murray at the Raleigh Farmers Market.

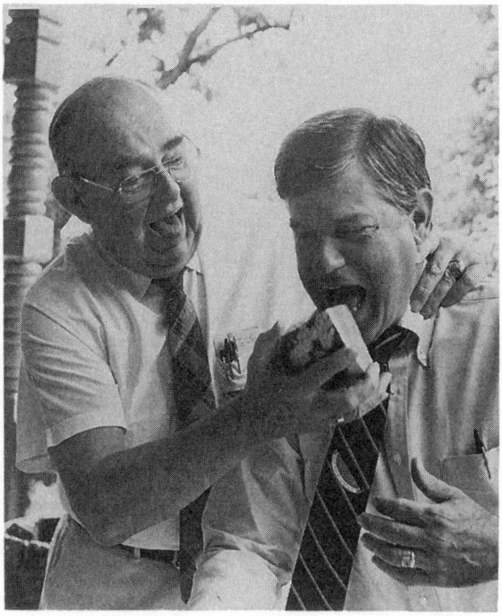

TOP: With Governor's Dan K. Moore and Robert W. Scott on the day of their Inauguration. CENTER: With Governor Jim Martin at the Watermelon Festival. LEFT: With Governor Jim Holshouser.

TOP: Taking the oath of office for the first time in 1964 from Associate Justice Carlisle Higgins as Governor Terry Sanford and others watch. BOTTOM: With Governor Jim Hunt in 1993 at his 4th Inauguration, and with Jim Hunt, as a candidate for Lieutenant Governor in 1972.

TOP: Campaigning with Jimmy Carter in 1972 and Hubert Humphrey in 1968. ABOVE: With President Bill Clinton in 1992. LEFT: With Walter Mondale in 1984.

TOP: Breaking ground for the Jim Graham Building at the Fairgrounds as Jeff Suggs helps with the horses. RIGHT: With Senator Sam Ervin, Jr. and Secretary of State Thad Eure.

Commissioner Graham shown as the President of his Senior Class at NC State University in 1942 (center) with Robert T. Pleasants (left) Sec./Treasurer and H. Clay Ferebee, Vice President.

Chapter 9

32 Years on the Campaign Trail

The story of the "bray" heard around the world.

I have enjoyed campaigning for public office. There is no better way to get to know the people of North Carolina, to understand their particular needs and desires than to put your name on a statewide ballot and ask the voters for their approval. During my tenure as North Carolina Commissioner of Agriculture, and especially during the nine campaigns I've run, I have come to know the people of North Carolina as the best people on the face of the earth. They are good people, hard working, diligent and concerned about their families and their future. They will tell you what is on their minds and if you listen to them, you will know what government needs to do to serve them well.

I joined the Democratic ticket in a rather unusual way in 1964. Mr. L.Y. Ballentine, the incumbent commissioner had been re-nominated in the May Primary for another term. He died two months later and Governor Terry Sanford appointed me to the unexpired term. In the culmination of my life-long dream, I was sworn into office as North Carolina Commissioner of Agriculture, July 30, 1964.

There was a long parade of candidates who went before the State Democratic Executive Committee meeting early in the summer to select the Democratic nominee for the November ballot.

There were two campaigns to win in just a short period of time. First, I had to get the party's nomination and that was not easy with six other people wanting the job. Second, I had to raise money and put together a campaign for the fall election.

There was yet another complication that required great sensitivity on my part. In the primary election of 1964, the North

Carolina Democratic Party had just been torn by a divisive intra-party three-way fight among L. Richardson Preyer of Greensboro, Superior Court Judge Dan K. Moore, from Western North Carolina, and I. Beverly Lake, a Wake Forest University Law Professor. Preyer, the favorite candidate of Governor Sanford's people, led the first primary. However, the supporters of I. Beverly Lake, a Wake Forest University professor, worked for and voted for Moore in the runoff and that gave him the second primary victory. As an employee of state government under Governor Sanford, naturally I was loyal to him and that placed me in the delicate position of campaigning first for the party's nomination and second, for the entire Democratic ticket, headed by Moore in November. That campaign was my first introduction to "hard-ball" politics within the Democratic Party.

Governor Moore was elected with a comfortable margin in November and he became a good governor. In retrospect, it is unfortunate that North Carolina had to choose between Governor Moore and Judge Preyer, who later served a term in the U.S. Congress and was appointed to the federal court. They both were good men. I. Beverly Lake was appointed to the North Carolina Supreme Court by Governor Moore.

In my own campaign, in November, I faced Van Watson, a prominent citizen from Eastern North Carolina. He had been carefully picked by the Republican Party as an able and aggressive candidate to take on Mr. Ballentine. The Watson name is highly regarded among the farm community. That campaign, my first, was a very tough introduction into North Carolina politics.

I had saved a little less than $10,000 from raising and selling cattle in anticipation of the day when I would run for Commissioner of Agriculture. That seemed like all the money in the world then; however, today, it would buy only a few television ads.

My closest race was in 1968 facing Claude L. Greene who had been director of the Farmer's Home Administration in Martin County. He previously had gotten statewide recognition by running for the U.S. Senate against Sam Ervin.

The year 1968 was not a good year for Democrats. President Lyndon Johnson had decided not to run for re-election because of growing opposition to the Vietnam War. Vice President

Hubert Humphrey was the Democratic nominee for President and when he came to a rally at Asheville, North Carolina, other state Democratic candidates would not join him. Opinion polls showed that Richard Nixon would beat Humphrey in North Carolina, as he did. Apparently, other Democrats were afraid that if they got too close to Humphrey, it might hurt their campaigns. I joined Humphrey for his campaign appearance and I'm glad I did. He was a good man, though I thought at the time he talked too much. I won the 1968 campaign for Commissioner of Agriculture by 166,147 votes. That was my closest campaign. It is worth noting that Richard Nixon carried North Carolina in 1968, the first time a Republican candidate for President had won this state since we had made another big mistake in voting for Herbert Hoover over Al Smith in 1928.

My next opponent, Kenneth Roberson, ran twice. He was a gentleman. We each ran a high road campaign. I ran my campaign and he ran his campaign. We never mentioned each other. In the first campaign against Mr. Roberson I won by nearly 200,000 votes. Republicans won the Governor's race for the first time in this century in 1972 with Jim Holshouser, a member of the House of Representatives from Boone.

Nobody gave Holshouser much of a chance of winning until the final days of the campaign. Two factors contributed significantly to his victory. First, the national Democratic party was in chaos. The procedure for nominating our candidates had changed and that led to the nomination of George McGovern who lost to Richard Nixon in a landslide.

Second, there was a spirited primary campaign between Hargove "Skipper" Bowles, a state senator from Greensboro and incumbent Lieutenant Governor Pat Taylor of Wadesboro. Taylor had the support of the conservative wing of the party and Bowles' supporters included what was left of the Sanford coalition. Bowles's campaign team did not welcome Taylor's supporters back into the party after the primary and many key Taylor supporters worked openly for Holshouser and were appointed to top positions in his administration.

Campaign Vote Totals 1964-96

Year	Commissioner Graham	Opponent
1996	1,409,801	Tom Davidson 980,224 Eugene Paczelt (L) 24,217 R. Gaines Steer (NL) 25,052
1992	1,463,744 *(Led Ticket)*	Leo Tew 899,774
1988	1,182,800 *(Highest Democrat vote)*	Leo Tew 830,045
1984	1,202,951	Leo Tew 842,729
1980	1,102,719 *(Led Council of State)*	Unopposed
1976	1,053,650	Kenneth H. Roberson 460,735 Edwin B. Drury (Amer.Party) 9,017
1972	761,734	Kenneth H. Roberson 580,628
1968	787,179	Claude L. Greene 621,032
1964	803,373	Van S. Watson 498,364

Table 9

Holshouser won with a narrow 25,000-vote margin and became the first Republican Governor of North Carolina elected in this century. Elected lieutenant governor that year was a young Wilson County lawyer named Jim Hunt who was laying the foundation for a future political dynasty. 1972 was also the first time Jesse Helms was elected to the U.S. Senate.

In 1976 Democrats prevailed everywhere. We even carried Wilkes County and I had to keep a campaign promise I never thought possible--kissing the rear end of a jackass in public. President Nixon had resigned in disgrace, facing almost certain impeachment for the Watergate crimes if he didn't get out of town. Mr. Roberson ran against me, again, and I won by nearly 600,000 votes. That was the first time I got more than a million votes and that was the first time my friend, Harlan Boyles, ran and was elected State Treasurer. We became good friends then and that friendship had continued and grown stronger over the years.

The "Bray" Heard Around the World

Jimmy Carter was the Democratic Party's nominee for President in 1976 and we were proud of him. He was a Southerner and a farmer. I didn't want to make a boring speech when it came my time to speak while campaigning with him in Greensboro, so I did my "donkey bray." It brought down the house and Carter loved it. Network television crews picked up my "donkey bray" standing beside Jimmy Carter and it was broadcast around the world. I got cards, letters and telephone calls from everywhere about that incident. I liked President Jimmy Carter because he was a farmer. He understood the special needs of the farmer and he appreciated what the farmer has done for this country. President Carter was a good and honest man. He did more to protect and preserve the dignity of the office of President than many before him and after him.

I did the "donkey bray" in my very first campaign in 1964. All of the statewide Democratic candidates were campaigning together in a bus tour of the state. Governor Moore had promised to visit every county and we were taking the bus across the state, stopping at each courthouse for a rally. One night we had left Alleghany County and the bus was making its way across those crooked mountain roads toward the western part of the state. As we approached Haywood County, Dan Moore realized that everyone on the bus except himself and me were asleep. He asked me, "Jim, do you think you can wake up this crowd?"

I let out my first "donkey bray" and everybody came alive. I remember vividly, the reaction of then State Treasurer Edwin Gill and Secretary of State Thad Eure. Both were senior statesmen of considerable stature at that time. Mr. Gill had been Treasurer for more than a decade. Mr. Eure already had been Secretary of State for 30 years. I came to love and respect both of them dearly. Neither of them, however, were happy to be disturbed out of their sleep by the sound of a jackass, even if it was the beloved mascot of our party.

Later that year at the Vance-Aycock dinner in Asheville, the audience responded wildly to my "donkey bray." Mr. Gill came up to me afterwards. He said, "Jim, it just isn't fair. I spent weeks thinking about and writing my speech. They hardly nodded during the 45 minutes it took me to give it. And you had the crowd shouting wildly with nothing more than that damn "donkey bray."

I've already told how I got in trouble with the "donkey bray" in Wilson.

The campaign of 1980 will always remain a very special memory for me. Although I did not have any Republican opposition I led the ticket in November, getting more votes than anybody else. I considered that a vote of confidence from the people I served. Ronald Reagan carried North Carolina and was elected President.

My opponent in 1984, Leo Tew, would run three times. A commercial airline pilot, I'm sure he is a good man but he voiced some strange ideas in that first campaign. He had negative things to say about me but they didn't amount to much. The thing I remember most about Mr. Tew was his emphasis on organic farming. That was about all he had to talk about and I was told he sold organic fertilizer out of the back of his car during the campaign.

With Mr. Tew opposing me also in 1988, I was the highest Democratic vote getter and again in 1992, I led the ticket. Democrats lost the Governor's race in 1984 and 1988. Governor Jim Martin beat former Attorney General Rufus Edmisten in 1984 and he defeated incumbent Lieutenant Governor Robert Jordan in 1988. We lost the governor's race in 1984 because the party fell out over the bitter primary campaigns between Edmisten and

Charlotte Mayor Eddie Knox. We lost the 1988 governor's race partly because Governor Martin had done a decent job as governor and Democrats simply ran a poor campaign.

I remember affectionately the election of 1992 as the year I received the highest number of votes ever, 1,463,744 and led the entire ticket.

The year 1996 shall always be a high point in my political career. It was my ninth and, most likely, final campaign. I worked hard, despite early polls showing that I would win easily. I worked not only for myself but I worked hard for other Democrats on the ticket.

The Democratic Party

I want to say a word about the Democratic party. The Democratic Party has been good to me and I've tried to be loyal to the party over the years. I stood on the platforms with our party's nominees for President when no other North Carolina Democrat would do so. I appeared with Hubert Humphrey, Jimmy Carter, Walter Mondale and Bill Clinton.

The Democratic Party has done many good things for North Carolina. I am proud to be a Democrat and I shall always be a Democrat.

Like many other people I am somewhat disillusioned by the special interests that have gained power within our party. The Democratic Party served this state and the nation best when it came together for the good of all the people. Party leaders made a big mistake in the late 1960s when rules were changed to give a lot more say to the splinter groups that push a single, narrow agenda. Today, it seems the Democratic Party is made up of so many factions, each interested in only what the party can do for its cause. They are pulling the party apart in their attempts to force everybody else to adopt their narrow agenda. This is why, I believe, that many middle-of-the road, mainstream Democrats are leaving the party to become independent or Republican voters.

In spite of my concerns, I shall always remain a Democrat. I will always be loyal to the party that has served me and my fellow North Carolinians so well.

The Donkey

The donkey can trace its proud heritage as the mascot of the Democratic Party to the 1828 presidential campaign of North Carolina native Andrew Jackson. President Jackson's opponents called him a "jackass" for his populist views and for his slogan, "Let the people rule." Instead of shying from this association, Jackson turned it to his advantage by using the donkey on his campaign posters.

Democrats are proud of the homely but humble, surefooted, and loveable donkey as our standard bearer. His stubborn resiliency is a trait of which our country needs more. I love the sound of a donkey. Its bray is music to my ears.

(L-R, from top) With Andy Griffith; Former President Gerald Ford and State Fair Manager Art Pitzer; With Speaker of the House, Dan Blue; As a high school basketball coach; With then Congressman Martin Lancaster (now President of the NC Community College System); Opening another State Fair with Wayne Miller and the late Sam Rand; and With Hugh Morton of Grandfather Mountain and State Treasurer Harlan Boyles at Molly Broad's Inauguration as President of the University of North Carolina.

(L-R, then down) I Love My Job; With long time friend, State Treasurer Harlan Boyles; I'm proud of tobacco and what it has done for North Carolina; With Roddy Jones and Steve Stroud; and, With Jack Stackhouse, former Ohio Commissioner of Agriculture.